Living wi.

MW00679900

Advanced Praise

∽

In *Living with the Lid Up*, Kari has truly embodied the belief that you should bring your whole self to everything you do. That means to leadership, business, life—the whole package! She shares her personal stories with a humorous vulnerability that speaks to the soul of every working person. Kari knows and understands the power of storytelling, how it connects us and helps build relationships. With each chapter, you will laugh out loud and ponder the lessons learned. Definitely a fun read that reminds us we are only human!

—Lani Basa, CEO and lead facilitator, The BWC

Kari is a true storyteller when it comes to authentically sharing her experiences. What sets her apart is her application. I never would have guessed that Kari's life and times with her sons, Max and Sam, could impact the decisions I make in my business on a daily basis. A very entertaining and informative page-turner!

—Tara Schmakel, founding partner, Integrus Global

Kari brings a smile to your face on every page of her stories. But she also gets you thinking—and smiling—about your own. Positive and fun, *Living with the Lid Up* shows you how you can actually build your business and client loyalty through storytelling!

—**Nancy Giacomuzzi, executive director, BNI Minnesota and Northern Wisconsin**

Living with the Lid Up

Hilarious and Heartwarming Life Lessons
from a Wife, Mother, and Entrepreneur

by Kari Switala

Dyonne,

First, you have the best laugh in the world! You are bold and fun and ♡♡ it! thank you for being you!

♡ Kari

Living with the Lid Up

Hilarious and Heartwarming Life Lessons from a Wife, Mother, and Entrepreneur © Copyright 2019 Kari Switala

Printed in the United States of America

ISBN: 978-1-946195-35-7
Library of Congress Control Number: 2019932555

23 22 21 20 19   5 4 3 2 1

Photo Credits: Author photo by Shannon Tacheny
Creative Director | Brand Strategist | Photographer
FeatherBlueStudios.com

Cover photo: Dan Iverson with Anthologie | theanthologie.com

Cover Design: Rebecca Rausch
Neon Lizard Creative Graphic Design
neonlizardcreative.com/

Interior Book Design: Ann Aubitz
Fuzionprint| FuzionPrint.com

Published by FuzionPress
1250 E 115th Street, Burnsville, MN

This book is dedicated to all the women out there who simply need a little laugh or an opportunity to reflect on the fact that they are awesome—just the way they are.

Table of Contents

∽

Introduction

A Checklist and Hashtag
for the Shower

∽

B eing a wife, mother of two teenage boys, and an entrepreneur, my life is full of surprises and stories. I can say I have a unique outlook on life. Hence, the title of this book: *Living with the Lid Up.*

In particular, I know firsthand that *hygiene* is a foreign word and concept for boys between the ages of nine and thirteen. My boys were no exception to the rule. Every day (sometimes multiple times a day), I found myself reciting the same three questions: Have you brushed your teeth? Did you take a shower today? And when was the last time you changed your clothes?

Sound familiar?

At one point, I got so sick of asking these same questions that I contemplated creating an app where you could record such questions or reminders and schedule them to be delivered to your child's phone at key times during the day. Can you imagine how nice that would be and how much time, energy, and breath you'd save? We are talking hundreds of hours here, people!

I digress.

One day, I decided enough was enough—I was going to solve this hygiene epidemic once and for all. So I brought both boys to the negotiation table, and we came to an agreement. The boys promised they would shower or take a bath every other day, no ifs, ands, or buts about it.

I was thrilled. This agreement would finally put an end to my constant reminders and frustration regarding showers and baths.

Have I mentioned that I tend to be overly optimistic about everything in life? It's true. If you looked up *rose-colored glasses* in the dictionary, you'd find a picture of me, smiling and surrounded by rainbows and unicorns.

About a week later, I was walking down the hall just as Sam came out of the bathroom after a thirty-minute shower. I was happy to see he had showered . . . but it wasn't my first rodeo.

As we passed, I simply outstretched my arm and ran my hand over his head. *Weird,* I thought. His hair felt strangely gritty, which didn't make sense.

"Did you wash your hair?" I asked.

Instantly, he smacked his forehead. "Ugh! Mom, I *totally* forgot."

Picture for a moment the most dumbfounded look ever. Well, that was the look on my face.

"What do you mean you forgot to wash your hair?" I said. "You were in there for thirty minutes. What were you doing?"

Side note: It has come to my attention that this is not necessarily a question you want to ask a preteen or teenage boy. Enough said.

"Mom, do you know what I need?" he continued.

I rolled my eyes and responded with an unenthusiastic "What?"

Then Sam proceeded to utter words I never imagined I'd hear from a nine-year-old who couldn't keep his room clean to save his life or remember more than one task at a time.

"I need a checklist," he said. "For the shower. Then I'll know everything I need to wash, and I can check it off as I go."

Do you remember the dumbfounded look I referenced earlier? This time, I gave him an even more dumbfounded one. Just when I thought I had heard it all.

"Buddy, this isn't rocket science," I said. "It's pretty simple, really. You start by washing your hair, and then you work your way down to your toes with some sort of soap or shampoo."

Seriously . . . as I type this, I'm still awed by that conversation.

I have told this story hundreds of times when out with friends and in front of large audiences. When I share the story, this is typically where I end it.

But wait—there's more!

Some, but not all audiences, hear the rest of the story. My incredibly comical and charming son continued this conversation without missing a beat or realizing I was still trying to pick my jaw up off the floor due to his checklist suggestion.

"You know, Mom, I feel really sorry for Dad."

At this point, I wasn't sure I wanted to hear more, but I'm a glutton for punishment, so I responded, "Why, buddy?"

"Well," he said, "I always remember to wash *one* part of my body—my butt!" Then he got this wicked glint in his eyes and a smirk on his face. "Have you ever heard of the credit card trick?"

Now, I knew this was a trap and that it would likely result in me feeling sick or seriously disturbed. But curiosity got the best of me.

"No. What is it?"

Sam decided it would be best to *show* me the credit card trick. So he went into the bathroom, grabbed the bar of soap, and turned his backside toward me. Then he turned and held the soap vertically and mimicked sliding it between his butt cheeks while saying, "Cha-ching!"

Oh, my God. For the record, my jaw dropped all the way down to the basement. I didn't know whether to laugh, cry, or call my mother. I mean, who comes up with this stuff? Did he see it on YouTube, or did he simply have an overly creative mind and a wicked sense of humor?

"Wait," I said, suddenly realizing there was more to the credit card trick than just that "helpful" demonstration. "You said you feel bad for Dad. Why?"

"Well, you see, I typically like to take showers in your bathroom before Dad does."

In that moment, I'd never been so happy to be an early riser who loves shower gel. I'd also never laughed so hard in my life. I couldn't wait to tell my husband, Kevin.

As if reading my mind, Sam winked and said, "Hashtag, credit card trick!"

Living with the Lid Up
Lesson
∽

Did that story resonate with you because you have a son or brother who also battled with hygiene? After hearing that story, do you feel we've got something in common or that you know me better? You likely answered yes to one or both of those questions, didn't you?

That's how stories work. Stories help us connect with people on an emotional level, whether they're funny, serious, or intense.

I wrote this book because I'm on a personal mission to erase the line between personal and professional and to show business owners and professionals how sharing their personal stories can help them connect and cultivate relationships with their customers, prospective customers, and employees too.

Stories are powerful. Stories are part of what binds us together. We've been telling stories as long as humans have been in existence. Even cavemen likely communicated through story.

Stories connect us to our listeners. When we share our own real-life stories, especially in business settings, people see us as authentic. Remember the old adage that people buy from people they know, like, and trust? It's true. Researchers have proven it over and over again.

This book is a collection of stories from my life as a woman, wife, mother of two boys, and an entrepreneur. My hope is that after you read it, you'll be inspired to start incorporating stories into your daily business interactions. Once you do, I'd love to hear about the impact it has had on you, your relationships, and your business.

Please note: if sharing your personal life is incredibly scary for you, perhaps because you're a very private person, then start small. Maybe you start by including a picture of yourself engaging in one of your favorite hobbies in your next newsletter. Or you could incorporate stories into your staff meetings.

However small you start, I can guarantee that you won't stop. That's because you'll see the amazing effect it will have on you, your relationships, and your business.

As I mentioned at the beginning of this chapter, I've told this story about my son hundreds of times. (Or at least most of it—not everyone hears about the credit card trick.) I've gotten some incredible responses.

For example, I told this story—in full—to a small group of peers at the bar after a business conference. In particular, Ben found this story hysterical, and he began talking about all the crazy things his two boys had done. Prior to this conference, Ben and I had been only acquaintances. We knew each other, but we hadn't really talked much. However, after telling him my story and then hearing him share his, we formed a connection.

The next morning, Ben surprised me with a fresh bar of soap from his hotel room with "#creditcardtrick" written on it. Hilarious! In fact, over the next few days of the conference, everyone who had heard the story that night brought me their fresh bars of soap to take home to my poor, unexpecting husband.

So, as you read this book, I hope you enjoy my stories as well as the *Living with the Lid Up* Lessons that help show how these personal stories relate to the professional world.

Most of all, I hope my stories inspire you to share some of your own. I hope you take a moment to jot down some of your memorable stories, then think about how you can use them to connect with others and start building deeper, more meaningful relationships.

Chapter 1

Shit Happens

∽

For Father's Day, I decided to surprise my dad with a family photography session at the farm where he grew up. So my mom, dad, brother, sister-in-law, and our family drove to Atwater, Minnesota, for our photo session with my dear friend and photographer, Dan. My cousin Justin; his son, Mason; and my aunt Sandy were there to greet us and give us tips on where we could find some good photo locations.

It was a picture-perfect day—no pun intended. But have you ever coordinated a family picture with young kids? If so, then you feel my pain. I think I could write a whole other book on the trials and tribulations of family pictures.

Anyway, after getting the boys dressed in their black T-shirts and denim shorts (each family was color coordinated, of course), I gave them the following lecture:

- Please smile nicely for Dan.
- Please stay clean until all the pictures are done.
- Please behave. If you do, this will be over fast.

Now, these are pretty straightforward instructions. However, for four- and six-year-old boys, these are tough rules to follow—especially when you're at a farm with animals and lots of poop.

Fortunately, they did pretty well. We were able to capture some amazing pictures of my dad and the boys driving the tractor as well as photos of the whole family exploring the farm.

As picture time came to an end, the boys waited longingly to hear me say the magic words: "Okay, you can get dirty now!" What I meant was, *You don't have to be so careful now that pictures are done.* What I *didn't* mean was, *I want you to get as dirty as possible.*

I guess I should've been more specific.

Within seconds, the boys took off with one of my cousin's kids to explore the farm. They spent over an hour checking out all the cows and farm equipment.

Then all of a sudden, we heard outrageous bouts of laughter. Being the mother of two boys, I know laughter *that* hard usually means they're doing something they shouldn't be doing. I also know it usually results in some good photos for their scrapbooks.

Nonetheless, imagine my surprise when I found the source of that laughter: the three boys were lying in the manure runoff, making snow angels—without the snow.

"This is the best day ever!" they exclaimed.

All I could think was, *They won't be laughing anymore once they find out that's shit.*

"Do you know you're rolling in cow poop?" I asked as I pinched my nose to avoid the stench.

"Yes!" all three of them said in unison. They began laughing hysterically again.

Once again, I was left amazed by the male species.

Naturally, my two dogs—Steve the puggle and Shelby the beagle—were inspired by the boys and decided to join the fun. I couldn't wait to ride home in the car for two-plus hours with two kids and two dogs who had been rolling in manure.

Fortunately, my aunt Sandy came to the rescue. While I took care of the dogs in our camper shower, Sandy took all three boys to the milk barn to hose them off and remove a layer of stench. The boys squealed with delight at the ice-cold water on their skin while they danced in their little tighty-whitey superhero underwear. I couldn't help but laugh with them.

Remembering how my boys equated rolling in shit to *the best day ever* still brings me great joy. To most people, just stepping in a pile of poop could ruin their entire day.

It's really a matter of perspective, isn't it?

Living with the Lid Up

Lesson
∾

Speaking of putting things into perspective . . . have you ever had a challenging client or employee?

I recently dealt with a very intense PITA (i.e., pain-in-the-ass) client who really challenged me to embrace the meaning of perspective. This woman got so far under my skin with her unreasonable requests and demanding attitude that I just about lost it. And that's unusual, because I have *a lot* of patience.

Has that ever happened to you?

Fortunately, Kevin reminded me that this was business, and in order to get through this situation I needed to put aside my emotions and look at the facts. Granted, he told me this over the phone, and I may or may not have flicked him off. Hmm . . . maybe I *was* too caught up emotionally . . .

After a glass of chardonnay and a hot bath, my anger began to subside. I was finally able to see the situation through the client's perspective. I realized she was under a lot of stress. She was so anxious about launching her new business that she took her frustration out on me.

When you're in a challenging situation or dealing with a difficult personality, it's important to look at the situation from the other person's perspective. That usually means setting aside your emotions, rather than allowing yourself to get worked up.

I've learned that finding perspective can help you resolve a difficult situation quickly, without all the added stress and frustration. It's a good thing to remember whenever "shit happens."

Chapter 2

A Furry Fashion Statement

～

Do you remember *A Christmas Story*, when Ralphie's brother tips over with his snowsuit on? The poor kid is lying there on his back in the snow, rocking back and forth like a turtle or bug. He struggles to get up, but he can't, no matter how hard he tries.

That, my friends, is what we call the snowsuit experience.

But it doesn't end there. Now imagine getting a six-month-old and a two-year-old into snowsuits and then fastening them into their car seats. It's like trying to stuff marshmallows into a piggy bank. Needless to say, it's a struggle.

One particular winter morning, I got up early so I'd have plenty of time to feed the boys, dress them, stuff them into their snowsuits, get them into the car, and drop them off at my mother-in-law's house for day care. I had everything perfectly planned out, so I'd have plenty of time to make it to the conference I was leading that morning.

But everything on my perfectly-planned-out timeline went wrong. Max didn't want to eat his breakfast, get dressed, or do anything but run around the house half-naked. Meanwhile, Sam *was* eating like a champ . . . but little did I know, he would spit up all that food on me just a few minutes later. Hello, acid-reflux boy!

So I got Sam into new clothes and even managed to get Max into some clothes as well. Then I changed into a different suit so I'd still look sharp for the conference.

We were finally ready to hit the road. I threw on some shoes and stuffed Sam into his snowsuit and his car seat. Once he was set, I ran back inside to get Max and repeat the process all over again.

At this point, I was sweating profusely, despite it being five degrees below zero. Ugh! I grabbed my workbag and purse and ran out the door.

Halfway to day care, I realized I didn't even have a coat on. I couldn't believe what an idiot I was. How could a Minne-*snow*-tan forget to wear a jacket in the middle of winter? Especially me, because I am *always* cold. The only time I'm not cold, apparently, is when I'm running toddlers to the car and stuffing them in car seats.

As I laughed at myself, I began to notice a strange sensation: my feet were really warm. How was that possible? I didn't want to do it, but at the next stoplight, I forced myself to look down at my feet. Instantly, my heart sank into my stomach.

I wasn't wearing my heels. My feet felt so warm because I was wearing my black Mammoth Crocs. You know, the ones with the supreme fleece-lined stuffing that makes you feel as if you were walking on clouds?

This might be a good time to also mention that I have canoes for feet. Meaning, no one, at any time, thinks my size

10.5 feet are cute. (Just ask my husband, who tells me all the time that he didn't marry me for my feet.)

Now what could I do? There was no way in hell I could drop off the kids at my mother-in-law's, go all the way back to my house, and still get to the conference on time.

All right . . . think, Kari. How in the world can we get ourselves out of this situation? Can we possibly make it to Kohl's and back before the event begins?

I ran a few short calculations. First, I determined that I still hated math and numbers. Second, I determined there was no way I could make it to Kohl's or any store, find a pair of shoes, and still make it to the venue before the conference started.

With no other options, I did what I always do: I made the most of it. I knew I would *definitely not* win any fashion awards for pairing my Mammoth Crocs with my tapered-leg business suit, but I walked right into the conference anyway. (And yes, it did feel as though I were walking on clouds.)

Because embarrassing moments are not new to me, I found a funny way to tie the Crocs and my story into my welcome message. Guess what happened. People laughed. My audience connected with me on a whole new level. It was no longer an embarrassing moment for me. It was a relationship-building moment.

Living with the Lid Up
Lesson
∾

I think this quote, popularized by Art Linkletter and John Wooden, really sums up this chapter and many of the chapters in my life: "Things turn out best for the people who make the best out of the way things turn out."

I hope you have noticed the theme threaded through each and every chapter of this book: let's be human, let's make mistakes, let's be easier on ourselves, and let's enjoy every moment of life. After all, we get only one chance at this whole life thing.

Chapter 3

Escalator Yard Sale

∾

When the boys were little, I was really fortunate to have Fridays off. Every week, I would look forward to our next Friday Fun Adventure. On one particular Friday, I decided to take the boys to the mall.

I know—I'm a slow learner and a glutton for punishment sometimes. It's just that I'm an eternal optimist. For some reason, I thought if I made shopping "fun" for the boys at a young age, they'd grow up to be men who love to shop. I was wrong, but who can blame a mom for trying, right? (In my defense, I thought I'd have a girl someday.)

Packing all the supplies took what seemed like an eternity: diapers, formula, wipes, Teddy Grahams, toys, wipes, an extra change of clothes just in case, and—yes—*more* wipes. Then at last, my two-year-old, my four-year-old, and I were on our way to the mall!

The sun was shining, and the kids were watching *Shrek* as I happily drove my maroon minivan (yep, I had one too) to the Burnsville Center mall. *It's going to be an amazing day*, I thought. (Hello, rose-colored glasses.)

Once we arrived, I had the joy of getting my two little ones out of the car and into the double stroller while managing diaper bags, my purse, and more. I was a hot, sweaty mess. Still, I thought, *It's going to be a great day.*

And it was—except for the last ten minutes of the trip. You see, after a very successful shopping trip to Gymboree, the Children's Place, Old Navy, and countless other stores, I decided to reward all three of us with frozen yogurt sundaes from the Macy's deli.

Side note: I have a strong love for frozen yogurt. I often joke that if I had to choose one thing to eat before I died, it would be frozen yogurt. More specifically, a TCBY white chocolate mousse fro-yo sundae with raspberries and cookie dough. Seriously, it makes my mouth water just thinking about it.

And oh, man I loved that Macy's deli! I'm still bummed they tore it down.

Okay, rants over. Now back to my story.

The boys and I enjoyed our sundaes. Once Sam, my youngest, finished his and I finished mine, I decided it was time to bring our mall day to a close. It was just about naptime.

Now, I wasn't a nap-ninja mom. You know the type—the ones who have to be home at the same time every day so their kids can nap. However, whenever the timing was right, and whenever I saw an opportunity to make naptime happen—which meant I could have two uninterrupted hours to myself—I took it.

Max was still eating his sundae, so I decided to put him in the stroller and carry Sam. We were making our way to the elevator when the boys spotted the escalator.

"Mommy, Mommy! Can we go down the escalator?" they said in unison.

My sundae flipped inside my stomach. You see, escalators, strollers, children, and I don't go well together. I never took the stroller on the escalator unless my husband or my mom was there to hold the other end of the stroller so it didn't crash.

That said, I had an incident, even *with* my mom, one time. She and I took Max down the escalator in the stroller when he was about one. He was in the middle of a nap, and I didn't realize he wasn't strapped in. As the stroller angled down the escalator, he began sliding out. Naturally, my mom was right there to catch him. We laughed it off, but it was still terrifying in the moment and likely scarred us for life.

So you can imagine the internal conflict I was facing as the boys now excitedly begged for the escalator. *Do I dare take them down in the stroller on my own? Or do I give in to the flipped-sundae feeling in my stomach and just take the elevator?*

My stomach churned, but I tried to ignore it. Instead, I circled the escalator like a boxer eyeing up his competition before the first round. I heard the theme from *Rocky* begin to play.

You got this, girl! I thought. *Don't let some stupid escalator stop you from having the most amazing mall day ever. It's time to face this scary metal monster once and for all.*

So I went for it! With Max situated in the stroller and Sam held to my side, we began our descent. As the stroller angled down, Max turned and flashed me a toothy grin with frozen yogurt all over his face. He was so happy, which made me happy—until I realized I had a death grip on the stroller handle. My palms were sweaty, and my heart was beating so fast it could have burst out of my chest. Thank God we were halfway down!

Just then, as Max returned to eating his sundae, the clasp of the stroller's tray popped open. Max, his sundae, and all the stuff I had on top of the stroller (my wallet, keys, water bottle, etc.) went tumbling down the escalator.

Now, I know what you're thinking: *Didn't you have him strapped in? Didn't you learn your lesson the first time he flew out of the stroller on the escalator?* In my defense, I honestly didn't think he'd need it. He was big enough to hold on, and I had no reason to believe the tray would pop open.

But pop open it did. I must have screamed because all the perfume salesladies from the floor below rushed to our rescue. They helped Max to his feet before he arrived at the bottom, and they began collecting my stuff as well.

I was *mortified*. I silently kicked and berated myself for making such a foolish decision. In a moment, I went from Mom of the Year, doing things to make her kids happy even if it causes her grief or pain, to *That* Mom. Isn't it amazing how quickly you can transition from one to the other?

I felt a sense of relief as I saw that Max was okay. Thank goodness! But then I felt the laser-like glare of one of the perfume salesladies burning a hole in me. I wanted to tell her my story and why I went down the escalator with my stroller, but somehow I didn't think it would affect her opinion of me. So I simply said "Thank you," gathered my child and my belongings, and walked quickly to my car. On the way, I apologized to Max profusely.

"It's okay, Momma!" he said.

I wish the perfume lady could have heard that.

After I got the boys and our gear loaded in the van, I climbed into the driver's seat. When I looked in my rearview mirror, I noticed that the escalator had left marks on Max's forehead. They looked like a barcode pattern. Instantly, I burst into laughter.

And then I gave the boys a special lesson. "You know, boys—sometimes there are things we don't need to tell Daddy."

Judge all you want. I know that wasn't a good thing to tell the boys. But it's true! Sometimes there are things we can just keep to ourselves.

Naturally, though, when Daddy got home from work, the first words out of Max's mouth were, "Guess what, Dad? Mom dropped me down the escalator today!"

Of course, the barcode on his forehead made it difficult to deny.

Living with the Lid Up
Lesson
∾

Have you ever made a decision that left you with an uneasy feeling in your stomach? That's your intuition and gut instinct, people. Listen to it! That goes for strollers and escalators as well as business matters.

I once had that gut feeling about two potential clients. And despite our "no-jerk policy," I brought them on anyway. I thought maybe they'd change after a few months of us working together. I thought maybe they'd turn out to be delights and not the controlling, type A, nothing-is-good-enough type clients they appeared to be. I'm sure you've had one of those clients before, right?

You're probably wondering, *So why did you take them on as clients in the first place?* It was all about the money, folks. We were in a bit of a lull. My husband was worried about our business financials, which in turn worried me. So I ignored my intuition, telling myself I just had to suck it up.

Guess what happened? After about four months of putting my team and myself through a ton of stress and frustration, we parted ways with these clients. Was it worth the money? *Hell no*!

The moral of this story, if you haven't figured it out by now: Please listen to your intuition. It's almost always right!

Chapter 4

My Not-So-Magical Tree House

A year ago, Kevin and I were taking a walk on land we own in northern Minnesota. When we came to my favorite spot, we stood there admiring the tall white pines and blue skies. That's when a vision came to me.

"I have an idea!" I said.

To which Kevin groaned and rolled his eyes. "This should be good," he said.

I then proceeded to explain my vision: we could build a tree house here in the white pines. This could be a place where we could relax, read a book, write a blog, and more.

I envisioned a tree house similar to something on the show *Treehouse Builders*. If you're not familiar with that show, then picture the tree house from any of the *Swiss Family Robinson* movies or TV shows. You get the picture, right? Big. Elaborate. Expensive.

After I laid out my vision, Kevin said something I've heard only a few times in our fifteen years of marriage: "I think that's a great idea!"

Once my initial shock wore off, I checked to see if he was feeling alright. He confirmed that yes, he was fine, and yes, he was actually on board with this tree house idea. As we walked back to our cabin, we excitedly created a verbal checklist of the items we would need for the project.

The next weekend, Kevin began building the tree house. Each weekend after, he would make countless trips back and forth to the build site. He told me he couldn't wait for me to see it once it was done. The entire time, I was ecstatic. I pictured myself drinking a glass of Kendall-Jackson chardonnay while reading my new Lorna Landvik book and enjoying the gentle breeze through the trees.

After several weeks of hard labor, Kevin asked me to come and check out his progress. He said the tree house was nearly complete. When we got about halfway through the four-wheeler ride out to the site, he stopped.

"Oh, by the way," he said, "I don't have the doors or windows installed yet because I wanted to get your opinion first."

This should have been a red flag to me, but my rose-colored glasses failed me again.

He fired up the four-wheeler again, and we continued our ride. We were within about two hundred feet from my "magical" tree house when Kevin stopped suddenly yet again.

"Oh, I almost forgot to tell you," he said. "I haven't put the roof on yet either, so maybe you could give me some feedback."

Now, you would think I should have noticed this sign too. But alas, I did not.

When we arrived at our favorite spot, he said, "Ta-da! What do you think? It's awesome, isn't it?"

I was rendered speechless. When I looked up, what I saw was a simple structure nestled between two tall white pines. It had a plywood floor and a two-by-four staircase. It wasn't the magical hideaway I imagined with gorgeous cedar walls, beautiful picture windows, and a wine cooler. It was a deer stand—a tree stand for hunting.

As a deer stand, it's incredible! (Just ask any hunter.)

As a tree house . . . not so much.

Kevin was thrilled, but I was disappointed. What happened?

THE REALITY...

Living with the Lid Up
Lesson
∾

Here was our issue: my husband and I had very different visions of and expectations for our tree house, yet neither of us clearly communicated that. And because neither of us was clear, we never realized we had very different visions and expectations—until it was too late.

This same scenario can happen when you're working with new clients or clients with whom you've just started to build a relationship. Think about a time when you found yourself (or *nearly* found yourself) in the same situation as I did with the tree-house-slash-deer-stand.

Do you clearly communicate what your client can expect from you and vice versa? Do you share the time frame in which they can expect to see results from your products or services? Do you share this information *every time* you bring on a new customer? And is there a *specific time* in your customer's journey when it is best to communicate this information? These scenarios are not just limited to new clients. They can happen *anytime*. Therefore, the key is to always make sure you're communicating expectations up front and that everyone is on the same page.

The next time you sign up a new customer, tell them this story and use it as the starting point for a discussion on communicating expectations.

Chapter 5

A Tale of Two Colored Feet

❝Look, Mama! I pink!"

I spun around in my desk chair to see Sam, my two-year-old, in the doorway with a big smile on his face and bright splashes of colors all over his skin.

Let's rewind about twenty minutes. It was bath time. I had run out of those tabs my sons loved to add to the water to make it change color, so I put on my marketing hat and got creative. A quick trip to my kitchen provided just the right solution: food coloring. Yes, that's right. I used food coloring to tint the bathtub water so my two boys would take a much-needed bath. Fortunately, the food coloring didn't stain my bright white bathtub because it was properly diluted in the water.

After a nice, clean bath, I put both boys in my bed to enjoy a cartoon while I caught up on a few emails in my office right around the corner. Apparently, though, the boys didn't stay in bed . . .

And that brings us to the moment when in walked my little guy wearing a diaper and SpongeBob shirt and with a variety of colors splashed all over his skin.

"Sam, what happened?" I asked. He led me to the bathroom to show me. He and his four-year-old brother, Max, had decided to climb up on the countertop, grab the food coloring, and empty the remaining contents into our white bathtub—without water. It doesn't take much to imagine the colorful masterpiece they'd created all over the tub, backsplash, tile floor, and themselves.

After a ton of cleaning and many Mr. Clean Magic Erasers, I got the bathroom back to its original state that night. But there was one thing I didn't realize until the next day at work, when I was sitting across the desk from a new prospect.

I was so excited to land an appointment with this big prospect that it took me a few minutes to realize he wasn't really paying attention to my sales pitch. He was too busy staring at my feet.

Now, my feet aren't exactly something most people want to stare at. I was wearing sandals that day, so I felt especially "exposed" as he continued to stare. After a few minutes, I had to sneak a peek myself. And when I did, my jaw hit the floor. The bottoms of my feet were tie-dyed! Apparently, the boys had experimented with the food coloring on my chocolate-brown rugs as well as in the bathtub. Lovely.

At this point, I wondered whether I should stop the meeting and explain why my feet were multicolored or whether I should just carry on as if my aspiring Picassos hadn't inadvertently turned my feet into art. I took a moment to weigh my options.

What the heck? I decided. *I'm a mom and an entrepreneur, and I'm going to embrace it!*

So I did. I turned my foot slightly and laughed. "Oh my! Let me tell you the story . . ."

My prospect and I laughed as I shared the tale. Instantly, the feeling in the room changed. We were no longer prospect and salesperson. We were two friends having a conversation.

I ended up landing the prospect. I know my story by itself didn't make the sale, but maybe it opened a door and helped form a connection.

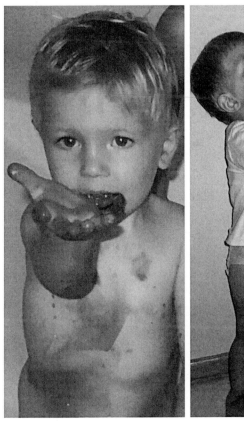
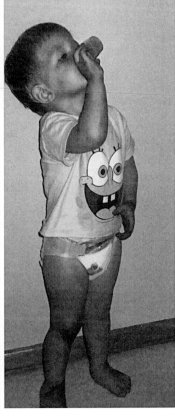

Living with the Lid Up

Lesson

∽

Let me ask you something: Why do we try so hard to keep our personal and professional lives separate? Are you a completely different person at home than you are at the office?

Actually, you're the same person at home and at work; you just act slightly different in these different worlds. Meaning, you (probably) don't scold your boss for not putting the toilet seat down in the office restroom, just as you don't negotiate performance improvement plans for your children after they've drawn a crayon mural on your living room wall.

I think it's time to embrace both our personal *and* professional lives and blend them together. After all, we're all human, right? How often do our personal lives affect our professional lives and vice versa? Let's stop stuffing things into separate compartments and just be ourselves!

If you agree with me, can I get an amen? If you're not a believer yet, that's okay. I'm pretty confident you'll be converted after a few more chapters!

Chapter 6

Breezy with a Chance of Massive Embarrassment

༄

It was the night before my *big day*! I had been hired to present to 350 Realtors who wanted to learn how to use social media to grow their businesses. This was one of my largest speaking opportunities to date. I could not have been more excited. Up to that point, I had hosted many workshops and spoken to dozens of organizations—but never 350 people. I had been practicing and preparing for a week. Now it was time to figure out what I would wear.

Some of you may be thinking, *What? You waited until the night before the big event to decide what to wear? What a procrastinator!*

However, a wise woman (who shall remain nameless) once told me that I'm not really a procrastinator; I'm just a business owner, wife, and mom who simply has too much to do. I must tell you, her words gave me a ton of relief. And actually, how can I be a procrastinator? I love checklists and time lines!

I digress. (Confession: I'm prone to tangents and "squirrel moments" that send me darting off in different directions.)

Anyway, when it came to what I would wear for my speaking event, I had one thing already figured out for sure: I would definitely wear my new make-you-look-skinnier-and-not-like-you've-had-two-boys-with-giant-heads Ruby Ribbon slip. I mean, a slip that's comfortable yet also sucks in your mommy tummy—who wouldn't want that?

So really, I only needed to decide on my outfit. After perusing my closet for what seemed like an eternity, I finally found *the dress*. It was a cute coral-colored tank dress that accented my summer-blond hair perfectly. I couldn't wait to wear it with my strappy sandals and turquoise jewelry!

Now all I had left was to pack my computer and get a good night's sleep, so I would be ready to rock the next day!

The next morning was hectic. Naturally, I had over-scheduled myself a bit, so I had to frantically work right up to the time I needed to leave for my event. After double-checking my bag for my computer and presentation materials, I jumped in my car.

Thankfully, my luck picked up at that point. I got to the event venue forty-five minutes early, giving me plenty of time to do another run-through of my presentation in the car. I was ready to rock and roll, baby! I applied one final coat of lipstick, and off I went.

Imagine my surprise, though, when I exited my vehicle and felt a gentle breeze in a place that should never feel breezy, unless I was skinny-dipping or living in a nudist camp.

Ladies, you know what I mean. In that moment, I realized I had forgotten to put on underwear under my Ruby Ribbon slip. My future flashed in front of my eyes: I saw myself walking up to the stage, tripping (which is a pretty common occurrence for me—just ask my family), and flashing my vajayjay (or whatever you call it) for 350 Realtors to see.

Now, I know some rock stars have had "wardrobe malfunctions" that led to massive publicity, exposure (pun intended), and, in some cases, new opportunities or popularity. Rest assured, if I were to have a wardrobe malfunction at this speaking event, I would've died of embarrassment *on the spot*! The headline would read, "Woman Dies of Heart Attack After Flashing 350 Realtors—Missing Panties to Blame." Yes, that would be my claim to fame and a news article I'm sure my parents would love to have framed!

How in the *hal-i-but* did I forget to put on my underwear? I can honestly say it's something I've never done before. Never. So why in the world did I decide to do it on my big day?

As I stood next to my car, it took everything I had not to call my contact for the event and tell him I had suddenly come down with a horrible case of the flu. Instead, I decided to suck it up. I planned to say a few million prayers before it was time to go onstage, and I would walk as carefully as possible.

I can do this, I told myself. *I won't let my breezy vajayjay get the best of me.*

So, I grabbed my computer bag and walked confidently to the front door. As I pulled the handle, though, the door was locked. That's when I looked around and realized there were hardly any cars in the parking lot.

Hmm . . . that was a bit strange. It was thirty minutes before the event. Surely the coordinators should have been there by now. I was honestly perplexed. I quickly checked my email and calendar to see if the event had been cancelled or if I were at the wrong location.

Looking at my calendar, I couldn't believe my eyes. I was so excited to present, I had somehow confused myself about the date. I was a week early! (See? I'm not a procrastinator after all!)

On my way home, I couldn't help but think, *Thank you, God, for helping me avoid what could have been the worst day of my life . . . but why in the world would Ruby Ribbon make a slip so amazing that it makes you feel like you're wearing underwear when you're not? Don't they know how many hats we women juggle on a regular basis? How are we supposed to remember to put on underwear too?*

Okay, okay. I guess that one was on me.

As soon as I got home and stopped laughing at myself, I added underwear to my list of things to bring when presenting. Then I texted my story to my friend, the Ruby Ribbon rep who had sold me the slip. I don't think I've ever seen that many funny emojis in a text message before.

Living with the Lid Up

Lesson
∾

What would you have done in this situation? Well, maybe not this exact situation. More than likely, you've never found yourself without underwear at a business event. However, you likely have forgotten, or will someday forget, something *really* important before a big meeting or speaking event.

This is definitely when our fight-or-flight reflex kicks in! So would you flee, or would you fight through it? Would you call in sick or make up some other excuse, or would you suck it up and go ahead with your event anyway?

As much as "sucking it up" truly sucks, if you do find yourself in a similar situation, I suggest grinning and bearing it.

One, we're human, right? And we're busy humans, at that. We forget things sometimes. If you forget something at an event, most people won't realize it. Even if they do realize it, they might be impressed that you had the courage to show up and do your best anyway.

Two, what if you bail and that speaking opportunity never arises again? Or what if you cancel on that once-in-a-lifetime prospect and they never call you to reschedule? Is it worth the risk?

And in case you're wondering, when the actual day of the event arrived, I did really well—and I *did* remember to put on my underwear.

Chapter 7

Holy Nipple, Batman!

∿

It was Mother's Day 2008. My husband was out of town for the fishing opener (which always falls on Mother's Day weekend—a guy must have come up with that idea), so I spent the day with my four- and six-year-old boys. It turned out to be a glorious day.

The best part is, apparently I had worn them out because they made a sleeping bag fort on my bedroom floor and fell asleep at six o'clock. That's right. I said six o'clock, y'all. Woo-hoo! Let's get this party started! (For those of you with kids, you know this *never* happens when you want it to, right?)

I stared at them, thinking about all the things I could get done now that they were down for the night. I considered hitting my to-do list. *But it's Mother's Day*, I thought. *I think I deserve a little pampering instead.*

So off I went to my bathroom (a.k.a. my oasis) to create my own spa experience. I found a cucumber facial, lavender bath salts, poppy-colored nail polish, and of course, the icing on the cake: a bottle of sauvignon blanc. This would be the best night ever!

First, I tied half of my hair into a high ponytail to keep it out of my face. I laughed when I saw my reflection. I looked a lot like Pebbles from *The Flintstones*.

Next, I applied the facial, turned on my steamy-hot bath, added a scoop of bath salts, and grabbed my book and a glass of wine. As I submerged myself in the tub, I felt the stress *literally* melt away. I promised myself I wouldn't wait till next Mother's Day to do this again.

After a steamy hour-long bath, it was time to wrap up my night at the spa by painting my toenails! I finished my second glass of wine as I applied the last coat of polish. I decided I should go to bed early, as I was feeling quite content. I corralled our two beagles and checked on the boys, who were still sleeping.

What a wonderful day, I thought as my head touched my pillow. *In fact, this might be the best Mother's Day ever!*

Suddenly, at two o'clock in the morning, I was jolted out of bed by the sound of an alarm. I thought it was my alarm clock, so I frantically tried to shut it off. Then I realized it wasn't my alarm clock but our security system.

Shit!

I jumped out of bed and ran over to the control panel. My heart was beating rapidly. The control panel lights indicated that someone was either trying to open or had opened the two sliding glass doors.

I instantly locked my bedroom door, grabbed my cell phone, and ran to the closet to call 911—all the while leaving the boys sleeping out on the floor. I know, I know. It sounds horrible that I left them there while I cloistered myself. In my defense, though, I ran into the closet so my call wouldn't wake them. Every good mom knows the rule about never waking a sleeping child, even in the middle of a potential break-in. Right?

Once inside the closet, I went into complete panic mode. As I tried to dial, my fingers shook, and I couldn't get my new iPhone to unlock.

Finally, I got through to the 911 operator and told her the situation. She told me to wait in my bedroom until the police arrived. She said she'd stay on the phone with me until they got there.

Even though I was in complete hysteria, I did have enough sense to realize I was wearing only a T-shirt but no pajama bottoms. I didn't really want to greet the cops in my underwear. Nor did I want to greet the murderer in my underwear—as I was sure there was one outside my door, just waiting to pounce with a big knife. (Did I mention that I have a very vivid imagination and that this scenario is one of my worst nightmares?) So I tiptoed to my dresser and grabbed a pair of shorts to put on.

I was still on hold with the operator, waiting for the police to arrive. Finally, after five minutes (which is an eternity when you think a homicidal maniac is outside your door), the operator said the police were at my front door.

I stayed on the line with her as I braced myself to unlock and open my bedroom door. Imagine my relief when the ax murderer of my nightmares wasn't waiting for me on the other side.

I raced down the stairs to see two male officers standing on my front step. I opened the door and told them what happened. One officer headed out back to check the doors and look for any disturbance. The other officer headed to the basement. All I could think was, *Oh my gosh. The basement is a disaster. I wish I would have cleaned it!*

After a thorough search, the officers determined there was no serial killer or ax murderer in my house. They wished me good night.

Right after they left, I turned on all the lights in the house and headed back upstairs. The boys were still sleeping soundly, having never stirred through the whole ordeal. And my not-so-protective beagles hadn't barked even once.

I started sobbing and violently shaking as the whole scenario ran through my head. As the tears rolled off my face and onto my shirt, I looked down—and broke into a nonstop bout of laughter. I was wearing my holy nipple shirt!

Let me explain.

My holy nipple shirt, as I referred to it lovingly, was my championship coed volleyball shirt from the University of Wisconsin–Eau Claire. It was my favorite night shirt. And as a result of excessive wear, I had worn a hole in the front that happened to reveal my left nipple. So the holey shirt turned into my "holy nipple" shirt. Yes, as in "Holy nipple, Batman!".

The horror and fear I had experienced that night was now replaced by laughter and embarrassment over the fact that the police officers likely saw my nipple. That and I had my hair stacked on my head like Pebbles. What a sight!

As I reflect back on that crazy night, I laugh and think that only a woman would (a) worry about how clean her basement is when there could be a killer hiding down there, and (b) be embarrassed about looking like a naughty version of Pebbles when the cops show up.

And by the way, I didn't sleep another wink that night because I thought the killer would come back to get me!

Living with the Lid Up

Lesson
∽

Why did I choose to tell you this story, especially when it references my nipple and doesn't seem to have *any* relationship to the business world? Because it's a good example of how we can deal with fear, anxiety, and embarrassment.

I'm sure you've found yourself in a scary situation at work before. Maybe you were afraid you didn't have enough in your bank account to make payroll. But after picking yourself up off the floor, you realized you'd simply miscalculated. Or maybe you showed up to an important networking event to meet your next big client, only to realize you were wearing one navy shoe and one brown shoe.

What do you do in these situations? It's easy—you *laugh*! According to mental health experts at HelpGuide.org, "Laughter triggers the release of endorphins, the body's natural feel-good chemicals. These endorphins then promote an overall sense of well-being and can even temporarily relieve pain"—or embarrassment, I would add.

Why not embrace your awkwardness or embarrassment and just laugh about it? After all, we are human, and we do make mistakes. Personally, I think I've earned my PhD in handling embarrassing situations. So don't take yourself too seriously, enjoy life, wear your mistakes like badges of honor, and just laugh!

Chapter 8

No Coat, No Gas, No Joke!

∿

Think back to when you were learning to drive. Likely, your parents taught you how to merge onto the freeway, how to parallel park, and how to avoid being *that* driver. Sound familiar?

Well, we learn all that in Minnesota, but we also learn how to pack a winter-survival kit and how to drive on icy roads and frozen lakes. Yes, it gets *that* cold here. My birthday is on January 16, so these two lessons were even more important since I took my driver's test in the midst of winter.

On my sixteenth birthday, I had an afternoon appointment at the DMV to take my driver's test. As luck would have it, we had freezing rain that day, and school was dismissed early because of the road conditions.

When my dad came to pick me up, he said, "Bub"—that was his nickname for me . . . I don't really know where it came from—"are you sure you still want to take your test? The roads are bad!"

Now, my dad had been giving me driving lessons for months. I'm sure part of him was worried about me passing, even without the bad road conditions. However, I was determined. I could almost taste the freedom. Bad roads wouldn't stop me from getting my license. No way, Jose!

Much to my dad's surprise, I did pass my driver's test and nailed my parallel parking too. Booyah! When the unhappy DMV clerk handed me that beautiful yellow piece of paper, I felt like Mel Gibson in *Braveheart*, when he charges into war shouting "Freedom!" Yep, now it would be just me and my navy blue Chevy S10 pickup, taking the roads wherever they might lead us.

Side note: Can you believe how many kids these days (that phrase makes me sound like an old lady . . . ugh) don't want to get their licenses? What in the world is wrong with them? Apparently, they like being chauffeured around town because driving themselves is "too much responsibility." I will never understand that thinking—ever.

Immediately after I got my license, my dad reminded me of two important things about winter driving:

1. Always keep a set of warm clothes, boots, and so on in the back of your truck in case you break down or get stuck in the ditch. In fact, Dad told me to put my winter kit together as soon as I got home from the DMV.

2. Always make sure you have more than a quarter tank of gas.

Now, I did hear both of those reminders, and I did take them to heart. But nonetheless, I was a sixteen-year-old girl who just wanted to take her truck for a spin *on her own*.

About a month later, I was getting ready for evening volleyball practice when I realized I was running late. I was already dressed in my shorts, T-shirt, shoes, and of course kneepads, so I just jumped into my truck and took off in a flash. No coat, no nothing.

Practice finished a little later than normal, so I didn't head home until around nine thirty. It was dark and about ten degrees—and I was still in only my volleyball gear.

As soon as I turned on the engine, I remembered that I was almost out of gas. *Dang!* I thought. *I better get gas, or I might not make it home. And even if I do make it home, Dad will kill me when he sees my tank is on E!*

Unfortunately, I didn't quite make it. I ran out of gas about a half mile from the gas station.

Ugh! How could I be so stupid? I chided myself. *Why didn't I listen to dear ol' Dad? Now, I have to suck it up and call him for help.* I knew I might as well buy a CD with my dad saying "I told you so" a thousand times, because I would hear that phrase over and over for the next several months.

So I took my cell phone out from under my seat and called my dad.

Another side note: Yes, some of you might be confused. If you're around my age, you probably assumed this was the typical 1990s, life-before-cell-phones story. On the other hand, if you're twenty-five or younger, your brains can't fathom life without cell phones, so of course you assumed I had one.

You see, back in the good ol' days (hello again, old lady), cell phones did exist, but they were not yet mainstream. Only a few people had them. My cell phone was actually in a case the size of a modern MacBook. In order to use it—which, according to my dad, was only supposed to be in an emergency—you had to unzip it, plug it into your cigarette lighter, pull up the antenna, and then dial the number. If my boys saw it now, they'd definitely think it (and I) was prehistoric.

My dad answered on the third ring. I did my best to sound as pathetic and apologetic as possible.

"Dad . . . ? I am *really* sorry to call you, but I was leaving volleyball and realized I was almost out of gas. I tried to get to the gas station, but I ran out of gas anyway. I'm only in my volleyball gear too. Can you come help me . . . ?"

And then I waited.

Finally, my dad asked me one question: "Didn't I tell you specifically not to go below a quarter tank?"

"Yes, but—"

He interrupted to ask the second question, which I knew would follow. "And do you have your winter kit in the back of your truck, like I told you?"

"I know you told me that, and I keep meaning to pack it . . . but . . . no. I don't have one."

Then my dad said something I'll never ever forget: "Well, Bub, I guess you better start walking to the gas station. When you get there, get a gas can, fill it up, and then walk it back to your truck and fill it up."

"*What?* Dad—wait!" I frantically responded. "You can't leave me here all alone to walk to the gas station! What if someone tries to pick me up?"

Dad didn't miss a beat. "Well, don't talk to them, and you'll be fine."

I was stunned and quite pissed too. *How can he do this to me? An ax murderer could try to pick me up. Or I could freeze to death. Or, or, or . . .*

I think the fury overtook my body and gave me the adrenaline rush I needed to walk my butt to the gas station. Along the way, someone pulled over and offered me a ride. As much as I wanted to get back at my dad, I was smart enough to decline the ride. I had to do this on my own.

When I finally got home, I was *flaming*. As teenage girls do, I stomped down the stairs and into my room, then slammed my door. I vowed not to talk to my dad for at least a year.

The next morning, though, my mom filled me in on the whole story. After getting my call, Dad (who has always been a big softie) jumped in his truck and drove to a parking lot halfway between my truck and the gas station. So while I fought the elements during my one-mile-round-trip walk, he sat in his nice, warm truck and watched over me. He wanted to be sure I was safe—however, he also wanted to be sure I learned my lesson.

Hearing this, I was both thankful and livid at the same time.

Looking back, I can honestly say my dad played that one pretty well. As a parent myself, I think it's so important to teach our kids both independence and responsibility, and that means not bailing them out all the time. After all, how else will they ever learn?

Living with the Lid Up
Lesson
～

Did your parents ever teach you a lesson like this? If so, did you learn from it? Have you tried to teach your kids similar lessons?

There's more here than a parenting lesson. I think this story is important to keep in mind while training your employees. They too often need guidance, especially when they are new. They likely need to hear things more than once, and they might make the same mistake more than twice.

However, the key here is that you can't bail them out every time. You can't, in essence, pick them up when they run out of gas and are only wearing shorts in the middle of winter. If they get themselves into a tricky situation, use it instead as an opportunity for them to learn independence and responsibility.

After all, isn't that what we want—employees who are passionate and willing to jump in, make some mistakes here and there, learn from them, and eventually take things off our plate? Use mistakes as opportunities to educate and elevate your employees.

By the way, I have a confession: While I did truly learn from my dad's lesson, I've never fully bought in to the rule about never letting my gas go below a quarter tank. Apparently, I like to live on the edge. I still enjoy finding out how far I can drive my truck until it's truly empty!

Chapter 9

Just a Minute Too Late

∽

One of my top-five favorite RV road trips of all time was when Kevin, they boys, and I went to Michigan with my parents, my brother, and his girlfriend. I know that doesn't sound super exciting. Honestly, when I first heard we were going to Michigan, I thought, *Wow. Michigan. That sounds like fun. (Not.)*

But as it turned out, Michigan was amazing. We went to the Upper Peninsula—the UP—and that was absolutely gorgeous. We also spent time in Traverse City (you should see all the wineries there), Mackinac Island (which is incredibly beautiful and doesn't allow cars), and Indian Lake State Park too. I guess what I'm trying to say is, if you haven't been there, I would definitely suggest adding Michigan to your list.

But I digress—that was a squirrel moment! I'm going to remove my tour-guide hat now and get on with the story.

While we were in the UP, we decided to check out this cool state park that bordered Lake Michigan. After looking at the trail map, we knew it would be a bit of a hike for Max and Sam, who were four and two at the time.

Before we hit the trail, we hit the potty. It was a vault toilet—the type you commonly find in wilderness parks. I took

Max in with me, because we moms *always* have to pee, right? I finished up, and then it was Max's turn.

Unfortunately, Max hadn't experienced this type of toilet before. It was a new experience to see nothing more than a toilet stool perched atop a deep hole, where all the poop, pee, and toilet paper land. Gross!

I get it. These toilets used to freak me out as a kid too. I used to think, *What would happen if you fell in there? [Insert gagging face and gurgling noise.] How would you get out? How unbelievably disgusting would that be?*

I think Max had some of those same thoughts. Instantly, he said he didn't have to pee.

Darn it! I reminded him that he wouldn't be able to go again for a long time. Still, he said he didn't have to pee. Personally, I think he was contemplating never peeing again.

Off we went to explore this beautiful park and its four-mile-round-trip trail.

About a mile into our hike, Max suddenly said, "I think I have to poop!"

There was a worried look on his face, and he placed his hand on his stomach. I couldn't quite tell if he was experiencing pain or if he was just terrified about having to use that dreadful vault toilet.

Good ol' Uncle Brent offered to carry him back to the toilet at the trailhead, while the rest of us continued on to see waterfalls, amazing wildlife, and wildflowers. Brent and Max met up with us shortly after we made it to our final destination, Lake Michigan.

Actually, I was a bit surprised that they caught up to us so quickly. That's when Brent told me that Max got "stage fright" as soon as he saw *that* toilet again. Brent did his best to sell Max on the comfort of the seat and how "cool" it was to hear your poop splatter, but Max wanted nothing to do with it.

All I could think was, *Oh boy. This might get interesting.* After all, how long could he really hold it in? Would he have to go on our way back? The toilet was two miles away now. To a four-year-old who suddenly needs to poop, it might as well have been two hundred miles away.

I took a deep breath and decided we'd cross that bridge when we got there. Instead of worrying, I focused on simply enjoying our trip. The boys giggled nonstop for over half an hour while we took turns skipping rocks on Lake Michigan. It was such a special moment. I even captured a picture of Kevin holding both of the boys' hands while looking at the lake. It was precious.

And that right there, my friends, should have been the warning sign that something was about to go wrong.

We decided to head back before the boys got too tired. As we approached mile three of our four-mile hike, Max got that same look on his face. I asked him if he was okay.

This time, he didn't even speak. He just shook his head.

Uh-oh! I thought. Actually, it was more like, *Oh shit! What the hell are we going do now?*

"Why don't you and I walk a little faster so we can get you to the bathroom as soon as possible!" I told him.

He nodded, and off we went. I cast a worried look back to Kevin.

About two minutes into our brisk pace, Max said, "Mom, I need to stop for just a minute!"

Oh crap! And I meant that almost literally.

I watched Max carefully. You know the feeling—the one where you have to clench your butt cheeks while you grimace and wait for the cramp to pass. Fortunately, it did. But just a few minutes later, he had to stop again.

This story will not have a clean ending, I thought.

We began to walk a bit faster, then I spotted the bathroom from afar. It was only a short walk away. *We might just make it in time*, I thought.

But suddenly, Max came to an abrupt halt, tugging my hand so hard it almost popped my shoulder out of joint. We waited again for the cramp to pass.

"Why don't I just carry you, so we can get there faster?" I asked.

He graciously agreed.

Well, have you ever tried to carry a child who's about to shit his pants? It's actually quite challenging. You have to keep them straight, to avoid any bending or early release.

We were just a few steps away from the toilet when Max said rather urgently, "Mom, please put me down for just a second."

Reluctantly, I put him down.

And then he said the words I'd been dreading: "Mom, I just need to fart!"

"Buddy, I don't think that's a good idea," I pleaded. "Just be still, and it will pass. We're right at the bathroom and—"

Then it happened. I heard it, saw it, and smelled it. At the same time, a huge grin appeared on Max's face.

"Ahhhhh! That feels much better, now that I pooped my pants!" he said blissfully.

This might be a good time to mention that I am not fond of poop. I'm okay with poop in the toilet and poop in the diaper. But outside of that, I can't handle it. I have been known to throw away *anything* that gets poop on it.

I reluctantly grabbed Max's hand as we did the "walk of shame" to the bathroom. (Just to clarify, I don't mean the "walk of shame" you and I might have done in college.) I helped him remove his super-cute red swim trunks with the bright-yellow Hawaiian flowers. I just about puked—poop was everywhere. [Insert gagging.]

I did the best I could to clean up my little guy, then I heard a knock on the door. It was Kevin, coming to see if he could help. (Great timing!) I told him he needed to find something for Max to wear. He couldn't walk out half-naked, as there were tons of people in the picnic area just beyond the bathroom. I didn't want my little buddy to be embarrassed.

After what seemed like an eternity, Kevin returned with a pair of red jammie shorts. You know—the tight ones that look so cute on their little butts. Unfortunately, these shorts would be extra tight and not-so cute because they were Sam's.

Instantly, I imagined Max walking out of the bathroom, in front of hundreds of people, wearing his brother's bright-red jammie shorts that were at least two sizes too small. As if crapping his pants hadn't been bad enough.

This will scar Max for life, I thought. My stomach churned more than it had while cleaning up the poop.

Kevin didn't need to be a mind reader to know what I thought about Max wearing those jammie shorts in public. Apparently, the look of horror on my face spoke volumes.

In return, Kevin gave me the look that said, *Really? You're going there?*

He then turned and smiled at Max. "Just put them on, buddy. They're cool!"

Max eagerly put on the too-tight jammie shorts, then walked out into the parking lot with me. When we got to the truck, I expected him to say, "Mom, can you please find me something else to wear? That was *so* embarrassing!" But he didn't.

Instead he said, "Mom, these shorts are *so* comfortable. I want to wear them for the rest of the day!"

Mic drop!

Living with the Lid Up

Lesson
ॐ

There are a few lessons in this story, actually. The obvious one is about resisting necessary change—and how we typically land in deep shit because of it. There are many ways that can happen in the professional world.

But the lesson I want to discuss is actually the one tucked away at the end of the story. It's about my reaction to the jammie shorts.

I was certain he would be mortified, having to wear those ridiculous things. But really, *I* was the only one mortified. I projected my feelings onto Max. I've done this about a zillion times with my kids, my husband, my coworkers, and my clients.

Have you ever found yourself in a similar situation? When your child didn't get invited to So-and-So's birthday party, did you assume your child must be crushed . . . but deep down, you were the one who was crushed? Did you then confront So-and-So's parent, fooling yourself that it was on your child's behalf?

When your employee took on a huge project, did you assume she must be nervous . . . but actually, you were the one who was nervous? Did you then micromanage the project, fooling yourself that it was on your employee's behalf?

Projecting + Assuming = *No Bueno*!

Why do we do this? I won't get into the psychology behind it, because that's not what this book is about. But here it is in a nutshell: when difficult feelings pop up, we find it easier to spin them onto someone else rather than deal with them ourselves.

Really, I just want to draw attention to this behavior. It's good to be aware of it in your personal and professional lives. Spend some time thinking about what you might have projected onto others. Recognizing it is the first step to reining it in.

Chapter 10

Girl, I Don't Mean to Be Rude, but You Look Like a Dude!

∾

I have cousins in Naperville, Illinois. Growing up, one of my favorite things to do when visiting them was to go to downtown Chicago. I don't know what it is about that city, but I fell in love with it the very first time.

Maybe it was because Oprah lived there, and I've loved Oprah since I was in fourth grade. My best friend, Jenny, and I would come home from school and watch Oprah's talk show as if we were two little old ladies. We loved every minute of it. (I've always been an old soul.)

My aunt and cousins knew how much I loved Oprah. So, every time we planned a visit, they'd try to get us tickets to be in the studio audience. Unfortunately, it never happened, despite their best efforts.

One time when I was in college, my mom and I planned a trip to Naperville. Sensing my disappointment about never being able to see Oprah, my aunt and cousins got us tickets to the next best thing: *The Jenny Jones Show.* No, it definitely wasn't Oprah, but I was excited and thankful for this adventure, nonetheless.

Before the trip, I told some of my guy friends about how I was going to *The Jenny Jones Show*. Corey, Lew, and Josh were thrilled.

"You've got to find a way to say something so we can see you on TV," Lew said, referring to how Jenny sometimes went to the studio audience for questions.

I've never been one to turn down a challenge. Just ask my college roommates, who had to drive me home after someone bet I couldn't do five shots of Phillips Hot 100 (yep, the cinnamon schnapps) in a row. Yes, I did win that one. In hindsight, however, I don't think spending three hours with your head over a toilet and having a massive hangover the next day can be considered a win.

The point is, I accepted Lew's challenge.

The morning of the show, my cousin Stephanie and I spent hours primping and searching for the best outfits for our first TV appearance. Then we and our moms took the train into Chicago. As we got closer and closer, the excitement kept building.

Upon arriving at the studio, we learned we had to go through "Audience School." Have you ever heard of such a thing? We learned how to clap, how to cheer, and how to make surprised looks. It was probably the cheesiest and most ridiculous class I've ever attended, but it was a necessary evil in show biz.

Once we finished our class, we headed to the studio, found our seats, and waited to see what would happen next. While sitting there, I thought about what Lew had said about me getting on camera. I couldn't wait to hear the title and topic of the day's show so I could mentally prepare some intuitive questions and thought-provoking comments for my TV debut.

Suddenly, the producer appeared on stage. We all clapped and cheered like the good Audience School graduates we were. I was hoping the producer would tell us more about the day's topic, but he said we had to wait until Jenny Jones announced it on camera at the beginning of the show. I was kind of bummed.

But then the producer asked for volunteers. Instantly, I shot my arm into the air.

Oh yeah, baby—it's gonna be a makeover show! I thought.

I *loved* makeover shows. How cool would it be to get a stylish new hairdo or get dressed in a super cute outfit I could keep afterward? Forget about getting on camera just to ask a silly question. I wanted to be featured with awesome before-and-after pictures as I modeled my new makeover. My friends would die!

As I was running all these supercool scenarios through my head, the producer and his assistants honed in on me and my raised hand.

Oh my gosh! I thought. *I think they just selected me for the makeover. Can this really be happening?*

Let me explain something—if you haven't already realized it at this point in the book: Luck and I don't have a great relationship. In fact, we've never really gotten along, except for on my eighteenth birthday, when I won one hundred dollars on the slot machines at Mystic Lake Casino. Other than that, luck has not been a friend I can rely on. So being chosen as a makeover volunteer on *The Jenny Jones Show* was nothing short of a miracle.

The producer then explained that Jenny would ask for volunteers during the live show. Those of us who raised our hands this first time were to raise them again, so Jenny could "randomly" pick us.

I could hardly wait!

After a few minutes, the producer began the countdown to showtime and cued the theme music. We were all excited, but we knew we had to wait for our cue to clap and cheer. Then, at last, the curtains parted, Jenny Jones appeared onstage, and we went wild.

After Jenny welcomed us, she finally revealed the topic of the show. That was when my heart sank. You see, the title was, "Girl, I Don't Mean to Be Rude, but You Look Like a Dude!"

Damn! Why did I raise my hand? And why did the producer and assistants hone in on me? Did they think I looked like a dude? *Me*, with all my makeup, long blond hair, and cute outfit?

Or maybe they hadn't honed in on me after all. Perhaps someone behind me looked like a dude, and I mistakenly assumed they had been looking at me.

Yep. That's probably what happened . . .

Jenny went on to introduce the day's guests: three women who looked or dressed like men, according to the family members who had nominated them for this show. The goal of the show was to give the three women makeovers, so they looked more feminine.

Ah! So that's why they need volunteers, I thought. *To judge who looks best after their makeover. Right . . . ?*

I tried to relax and enjoy the show as Jenny interviewed these three women, but inside, my stomach churned. Then the moment arrived: Jenny asked for volunteers to participate in a "fun project."

Remembering what the producer said about raising your hand, I did as I was told. But this time, my hand didn't shoot straight up. It slowly raised to half-mast.

Horrified, I saw them hone in on me again. Jenny walked right over to me with her microphone and asked my name.

Oh my God! I wanted to die. I nervously told her my name and where I was from.

That was when she explained what I had just volunteered for. As a twist, they wanted to show how a feminine-looking woman could be transformed to look like a man.

This . . . cannot . . . be . . . happening.

But it was. Jenny took my hand, led me to the stage, then turned me over to her makeup artists.

Yes, just wait till my friends—and the rest of the country—see this.

Then the "man-over" began. Let's face it—it wasn't really a makeover. Or at least not the one I wanted. But thanks to my dysfunctional relationship with luck, I've mastered the ability to make lemonade out of lemons.

So I decided to live it up. I have to admit, it was a pretty cool experience to be backstage. I had a blast talking with the staff members and learning the secrets of TV production.

They pinned up my long hair with a zillion bobby pins so I could be fitted with a short dark wig. Next, they removed all the makeup I had spent hours perfecting that morning. They exchanged it for darker foundation, and they used eyebrow pencils to create a unibrow, mustache, and day-old stubble. The wardrobe consultant selected my new clothes: a dress shirt, pants, and suspenders. The entire time, they had me turned away from the mirrors, so I could only imagine how I looked.

Jenny came back to see how the transformation was coming along. She was quite impressed with her team's work. She told me she would soon call me onstage for my before-and-after pictures. She wanted me to really ham it up and make the most of it.

All I could think was, *Don't worry, Jenny. I'm a master at hamming it up!*

As my big moment neared, the team wanted me to see the results. So they stood me up and turned me around in front of a giant mirror.

Holy crap! I looked like a cross between Charlie Chaplin and a scary guy who drives one of those unmarked white vans.

As shocking as it was, I realized I still ultimately looked like a woman. With relief, I realized maybe that was why they had selected me—not because they thought I looked like a dude but because they wanted to show how even a very feminine woman could take on a masculine look.

Then Jenny came to the dressing room to tell me it was showtime. As we began our walk to the stage, she reminded me again to ham it up. She said the audience would be shocked.

That's an understatement, I thought. *Mom, Aunt Janet, and Stephanie are going to fall out of their chairs!*

Jenny asked me to stay just behind the curtain until she called me out. Instantly, my heart started beating rapidly. *How in the world did I end up here? Why do these crazy things always happen to me?* All I could do was thank God for giving me a sense of humor and the ability to just roll with it.

Jenny reminded the audience about the "special" makeover, then asked me to come on out. So, I did what any creepy-looking Charlie Chaplin dude would do: I made a manly, macho face, strutted out onto the stage, and did a little dance with my thumbs hooked under my suspenders. I rocked it.

The audience went crazy cheering. And then the cameras panned to my family in the audience. The look on Mom's face was priceless. She was absolutely horrified! She thought they had actually cut my hair and dyed it black. Now, that is funny stuff right there!

As soon as I got home, my friends asked if I had gotten on camera to ask a question or make a comment. I told them I did something even better—I got *on* the show. They couldn't believe it when I filled them in on all the crazy details.

When the episode aired a couple of weeks later, we had a little viewing party. We all laughed hysterically about how ridiculous I looked and how funny my mom's face was when I came on stage. I must have gotten one hundred emails and phone calls from family and friends saying they saw me on TV.

It was an experience I'll never forget!

Living with the Lid Up
Lesson

Do you put yourself out there on a regular basis? Would you volunteer without knowing what it was for or what impact it would have? Or do you just sit back and watch others live it up, silently wishing you had enough courage to raise your hand? Imagine if you raised your hand and had an amazing experience that greatly impacted or changed your life. Wouldn't it be worth it?

I can tell you from personal experience that my answer to that last question would be, *Yes, it's definitely worth it!* I constantly put myself out there and volunteer to try new things. Are some of them fun and some of them painful? Yes. But that's the point. We can learn from both types of experiences, and those little lessons can have a big impact on our lives—personally and professionally.

As ridiculous as my man-over turned out to be, it gave me a special firsthand experience on a TV show, a great laugh for my friends and family, and reason to realize how lucky I am to be unlucky. And that, my friends, is why I raise my hand every chance I can get.

Chapter 11

Kevin Kicked Me Out of the Bed—Literally!

◌

I am one of those people who love to rearrange furniture and redecorate my house on a regular basis. In fact, the more time I have at home, the more likely I am to rearrange my house or change the paint color in one of our rooms. I've actually repainted rooms so much that Kevin jokes we're losing square footage.

One particular Saturday, Kevin had plans to go out with his friends to celebrate something or other. Side note: Isn't it amazing how many reasons men can find to celebrate (ahem—I mean, drink)?

I was excited to have some time alone to turn on HGTV, clean, reorganize, and rearrange. (I know . . . I'm weird.) After Kevin left, I immediately started brainstorming.

After several hours of cleaning and scheming, I decided to do something different with our master bedroom. I began moving furniture around until I found what I thought would be the best arrangement. The new layout provided not only more space but also a better view out our back window. I loved it, and I was sure Kevin would too.

Actually, I have to give Kevin a lot of credit. He's somewhat adverse to change in the house, having grown up with a mom who tended to leave things the same way forever. (I love you, Suzie!) And then this poor guy marries me, the girl who thrives on change and grew up with a mom constantly changing everything all the time. Needless to say, Kevin has adjusted and is now used to me and my somewhat psychotic behaviors.

I couldn't wait for Kevin to see the new layout. I stayed up a bit, waiting for him to come home so I could see his reaction. But as the clock ticked past the time he said he'd be home, I finally went to bed. I couldn't stay up any longer. I was disappointed—and, I might add, more than a bit frustrated—that he wasn't home on time.

So when I finally heard him come into the house, I pretended to be fast sleep. Nope—no action for you tonight, big guy!

I heard him trip over something downstairs. Obviously, he was somewhat intoxicated. I covered my mouth quickly to hold in a little giggle. Then it was back to pretending to sleep and silently assuming he felt bad for not coming home when he was supposed to. (Or not—it actually wasn't *that* late, truth be told.)

Kevin finally made it up the stairs. I heard his footsteps as he made his way into our room. He started to take off his shoes but lost his balance. Again, I covered my mouth to keep from laughing over the clamor of his stumbling.

Next thing I knew, I was lying on the floor.

What the hell?

As my brain tried to catch up, I heard Kevin giggle. I couldn't help it—it was contagious. I started laughing too. Our laughter continued for several minutes before either of us could even speak.

"What the heck happened?" I asked when we finally stopped laughing.

Kevin had to suppress another giggle before he could explain. Turns out, he had reached for the dresser when he lost his balance taking off his shoes. He didn't realize, of course, that the dresser was no longer there. So he fell backward. As he did, his legs flew up, and he kicked the mattress right off the box spring, which sent me sailing across the room and onto the floor.

"Oh my gosh!" I replied. "You just kicked me out of the bed—literally!"

Then the laughter started all over again.

Living with the Lid Up

Lesson

∾

We tell this story a lot because it's funny. But when I look back on it, I realize it represents the give and take needed to make a relationship work, whether personally or professionally. After all, no one is perfect. We bring our quirky behaviors and baggage to every relationship.

If you find yourself with a coworker or client you wish would change, I challenge you to find some middle ground. Instead of thinking about all the ways you want them to change, try focusing on even just one thing you like about them. This has helped me tremendously in both my personal and professional relationships. I think it will help you too.

God made us all different. If we were the same, life would be boring. We can't change who we are any more than we can change who others are.

We *can* change the layout of a bedroom, however. And that keeps life from getting boring too.

Chapter 12

Stick to What You're Good at, Mr. Stripper

ᨃ

Warning: If you skew a bit prudish, maybe skip this chapter. If you dare to continue, though, you'll get a kick out of this story and burst out laughing next time you hear someone clapping.

I bet you can't wait to see where this is going, right?

Well, it all happened at AJ's bachelorette party. AJ was one of my college roommates at the University of Wisconsin–Eau Claire. During our sophomore and junior years, six of us rented a house on Farwell Street, several blocks off campus.

Boy, did we have a lot of fun and make a ton of memories in that house. We formed quite a bond. After we graduated, we spent the next seven years attending one another's weddings and baby showers.

AJ was a lot of fun and open to most things—except for having a stripper at her bachelorette party. In the months leading up to the party, she told her older sisters over and over that she *really did not want* a stripper.

Of course, they told her that was not in their plans. They said we would play games, eat snacks, and drink fu-fu drinks before heading out to the bars in Green Bay. Sounded fun to me!

The night of the party, we gathered at the home of one of AJ's sisters. She led us all into the kitchen, where there was a ton of food, drinks, and laughter. It was a big group, with AJ's other family and friends in addition to us college roomies. It was such fun, we lost track of time.

Suddenly, the doorbell rang. We all looked around. Wasn't everyone here already?

With a terrified expression, AJ realized what her sisters had done.

Her older sister opened the front door, and two gentlemen walked in. The first was a rather beefy-looking guy dressed in overalls with nothing underneath, at least as far as we could see.

The second guy was the polar opposite. In his late thirties or early forties, he was prim, with perfectly styled strawberry blond hair. He was dressed in a full tuxedo. Let's just say he seriously needed to take a career-aptitude survey, because we instantly knew stripping wasn't his forte.

All I could think was, *This just got weird. Really weird.*

AJ was absolutely horrified when Mr. Strawberry Blond introduced himself and asked her to come sit in a chair in the middle of the living room. He said he had a "present" for her.

It became apparent that only Mr. Strawberry Blond would be providing the entertainment for the evening. Who knows—maybe Mr. Beefy Overalls was there as a bodyguard or for moral support or something.

AJ reluctantly sat in the chair, and we all surrounded her, including her mother and future mother-in-law. Zoinks!

This is when we got to experience Mr. Strawberry Blond's years of practice and perfectionism. He gyrated around AJ while removing his shirt. It took everything I had not to laugh at both him and the look on AJ's face. She was shooting daggers at her sisters.

Oh, did I mention that AJ's sister's house was in a quiet cul-de-sac in a nice suburban neighborhood? And that she had a humongous picture window without curtains in her living room?

Oh, and did I also mention that his whole body was waxed, and he apparently used a tanning bed every day, which left his nipples a strange pinkish-white color? (I know, I know. I probably just lost half of you right there. The rest of you, stay with me. It gets better. Which is to say, it gets worse.)

Mr. Strawberry Blond wasn't getting the catcalls and reactions he was expecting from a room filled with forty women, so he decided to take it up a notch. First he straddled AJ while she was plastered to the chair, sitting on her hands, paralyzed and mortified. Then he got up and removed his pants in a *unique* way.

Have you ever watched a gymnastic floor routine? You know how they square up their feet in the corner before they begin to run and flip? That's what he did—he walked over and squared his feet up on the corner of the rug before beginning his pant-removal routine.

Why, I don't know. Gymnasts square off in the corner to ensure proper footing, balance, and room before launching into a complicated series of moves across the floor. But all this guy was doing was taking off his pants.

Mr. Strawberry Blond was now down to only his bowtie and little bikini briefs. I'm sure he thought we'd start hooting and hollering while flocking to stick dollars in his aforementioned briefs. That's what typically happens with male strippers at bachelorette parties.

But that didn't happen here. This guy didn't even remotely fire us up. Worst yet, this guy didn't, um, *fire himself up* either. And therein lay the problem: he had to fire himself up if he wanted even a chance at firing us up.

By this point, AJ was about to puke. The way her eyes darted around the room, you could see her plotting her escape plan. Sure enough, she bolted as soon as Mr. Strawberry Blond removed his briefs and stood there in nothing but his bowtie.

But even without the bride, the show went on! The rest of us watched in awkward horror as Mr. Strawberry Blond added an ultimately unsuccessful "hands-on" element to his routine. All I can say is, at one point, there was a sound like someone rapidly clapping.

When we couldn't take it anymore, we burst out laughing and squealing as we covered our eyes. Several women took a cue from AJ and fled the room. Unfortunately, my friend Hogan and I were stuck in the corner.

OMG.

At last, the ordeal came to an end. With still no catcalls or dollars, and with only a few ladies left in the room, Mr. Strawberry Blond finally grabbed his clothes, huffed and puffed, and darted for the bathroom.

In that instant, the room went completely quiet, filled only with awkward silence. So we did what anyone would do in that situation: we bolted for the kitchen and began filling our drinks.

When Mr. Strawberry Blond emerged from the bathroom, AJ's oldest sister paid him the agreed-upon amount. He snatched the money.

"Next time you get a stripper, I would suggest y'all have a few more drinks first!"

That was it. He marched out the door with Mr. Beefy Overalls in tow.

Again, we exploded in hysterical laughter. Don't get me wrong—we did feel bad for him. It's just that the whole situation was so incredibly awkward and ridiculous that all we could do was laugh.

Given the shock of what we had just witnessed, we decided it was *definitely* time to hit the bars. While out on the dance floor with all the girls, I started clapping rapidly.

"Sound familiar?" I asked.

With that, we all began laughing once again.

Living with the Lid Up
Lesson
∽

I know it's borderline inappropriate to use such a risqué story as a launching point for professional advice, so I'll get right to the morals.

The first one is probably obvious: know your audience when sharing stories. This isn't a story I'd share in a professional setting. I wouldn't even share it in a happy-hour setting with work chums—unless I knew every person very well and knew they were all comfortable with sexual topics. If I thought even one person would be uncomfortable, I'd keep it mum. Stories should connect people, not alienate them. So think carefully about which stories you share with which people.

The second moral is built right into the title of the story: stick to what you're good at. This is especially key in business. So often, I see business owners completely switching gears or adding more services or products merely because they're all the rage. Like poor Mr. Strawberry Blond, they venture into areas they should *not* be in.

Growth is important, yes. But why not stick to what you are good at even as you grow? Why not focus on finding new and better ways to market your core services and products?

In particular, lots of companies push themselves into these ill-fitting areas because they're chasing someone else's success.

Why not be your own person and hone *your* skills and offerings instead?

The same is true for professionals too. Don't take on tasks well outside your comfort zone or skill level. All that will come of that is a lot of fatigue and frustration. Focus instead on what you do best.

Learn when to say "Yes, I can do that!" and when to say "I really wish I could help with this project, but I don't feel it's in my wheelhouse." Better yet, if a project is perfect for a coworker, why not share the limelight and recommend him or her instead?

Let me tell you—all of us ladies at that bachelorette party sure wish Mr. Strawberry Blond had recommended someone else!

Chapter 13

Pampered Chef Stoneware vs. My Ankle

At six o'clock on Sunday morning, I heard a little voice: "Mommy, I'm up!"

Yippee skippy.

You see, I was *exhausted*. On Friday, we had enjoyed an all-day-and-night extravaganza for my cousin Jeff's wedding. Then we followed it up on Saturday with Max's fourth birthday bash, complete with a snow-castle cake (Kevin is so talented—for your viewing pleasure, I've included a picture) and a five-hour tournament of yard games that stretched well into the night.

When I finally crashed after the party, I prayed the boys would sleep in, even though they were notorious early risers.

But apparently, God was quite busy answering more-important prayers that night.

I managed to drag myself out of bed and down the hallway to the boys' room at a sloth-like pace. I got the boys out of bed, and off we went to the kitchen.

"What do you want for breakfast?" I asked, silently hoping they'd say cereal.

No such luck.

"Let's have pancakes!" Max said.

Seriously? I could barely see straight, let alone make something as involved as pancakes. But alas, I wanted to stay in the running for Mom of the Year, so I went to the pantry to find the griddle.

Unfortunately, in my hasty cleaning and prepping for Max's birthday party, I had buried the griddle under a stack of other things. One by one, I lifted them, precariously shifting them around the pantry in a reverse game of Tetris to dislodge the griddle.

I was almost there when, all of the sudden, one of the Pampered Chef stoneware pieces crashed into the food processor. All I could do was cover my head with my hands and wince as everything on the top shelf—pots, pans, stoneware, and a food processor blade—rained down on me.

Kevin came running down the stairs in a state of absolute panic, then he just stared at me. "Are you okay?" he finally asked.

I surveyed the damage. I'd likely have a couple of bruises, but it wasn't too bad—except there was a nasty slice in my ankle. That and the Pampered Chef stoneware had been fatally injured—broken into dozens of pieces.

"I guess I'm okay," I said. "But something sliced my ankle."

Kevin mumbled what sounded like "Good. I'm glad you're okay." He then walked in a zombie-like state back up the stairs to our bedroom, leaving me and my bum ankle surrounded by the aftermath of the crash.

Hey, thanks for your help. I'll clean this up and *make pancakes. You just go back to sawing logs. Don't worry about it.*

Ugh!

I managed to clean up everything, making a mental note to never stack the items like that again. I served my princes their pancakes, then I sat down on the couch to take a closer look at my ankle.

Now, my husband would tell you I'm a hypochondriac . . . which may be slightly true. But damn, my ankle really hurt. It started throbbing. I could swear something was lodged in there—I could see it!

After an hour of my ankle absolutely throbbing, I came to the conclusion there *had* to be a piece of something in there. It might have been a piece of stoneware or a piece of metal from the food-processor blade. And because I couldn't remember the last time I had gotten a tetanus shot, I decided I should get myself to urgent care.

Otherwise, I could see myself looking back at this moment, thinking, *If only I had gone to urgent care, I wouldn't have gotten tetanus, and my ankle wouldn't have been amputated.* (Yeah, I might be a bit of a hypochondriac.)

I went up to tell Kevin my theory about something being lodged in my ankle and let him know he'd have to watch the boys while I went to urgent care. He gave me that look—like, *I think you're crazy, but I'm not going to say it.*

So off I went. After telling my story to the doctor and nurse, I ended up getting a tetanus shot, a couple of X-rays, and an appointment to consult with a surgeon at TRIA Orthopaedic Center the next day. It appeared I did have a foreign body in my ankle.

I called Kevin as soon as I got to the car. I couldn't wait to prove once and for all that I was right and that I was *not* a hypochondriac. He was a bit taken aback, and he apologized for not believing me.

The next morning, I went to TRIA. On my way there, though, I noticed my ankle didn't hurt as bad. I couldn't see the foreign object near my ankle bone anymore either.

The surgeon at TRIA confirmed that while there was a foreign body in my ankle, it had moved, which explained why it was no longer painful. He told me that, at some point, the foreign object might return to the surface. If it did, that would be a good time to get it removed.

Otherwise, if it didn't come to the surface, and if it didn't bother me, I could just let it be. The surgeon said that the same sometimes happens for gunshot victims. They often live with bullets in their bodies without any issues.

I have to admit, the ridiculousness of comparing myself to a gunshot victim was not lost on me.

Life continued without any problems until almost a year later to the date. That's when my ankle started hurting and I noticed the foreign object was visible again. I called TRIA, and they scheduled me for surgery the following day.

I assumed it would be a simple in-office procedure—a slightly more involved version of what I did when the boys got slivers. I was surprised, then, when they told me I'd still be medicated after the surgery and would need someone to drive me home. Kevin couldn't help but laugh when he heard this. I kind of agreed with him. It seemed like a big to-do for just a little piece of metal or stoneware.

At the hospital the next day, a nurse greeted me and took me back to a room. She told me to get undressed and into a hospital gown.

I gave her a confused look. "But wait—aren't they just going to lift up my pantleg, slice my ankle open, and take the piece out?"

She smiled. "Yes, that's more or less what they'll do. But it's very important that we keep everything in the operating room sterile. So, please change into the gown, and let me know when you're ready."

As I started changing, I thought, *Kevin will die of laughter when he gets wind of this. Come on—a hospital gown?*

The nurse came back in with a wheelchair—a wheelchair!—for me. She then asked me to tell her which leg was the one with the foreign object. I said it was my left. She proceeded to draw several *x*'s with black permanent marker on my left leg.

Oh my God. I was dying inside. I felt so foolish. This was *not* helping my reputation as a hypochondriac.

While she wheeled me to the operating room, she asked how this had happened. She laughed as I told her the story.

"Well, it will be interesting to see what they find in there," she said with another laugh.

At that point, I could only hope this piece of stoneware or metal was *really* big.

Now, I'd seen operating rooms on TV shows, but I'd never been in one before. Or at least not that I could remember. (I did have surgery when I was about six months old.) I was not prepared for the bright whiteness or the fact that there were three—count 'em, three—nurses and one doctor ready to operate on me. You'd think I were going into open-heart surgery.

They got me onto the surgical table and began the procedure.

"Okay, I think I've got it," the surgeon said after a few short minutes. "I'm just going to double-check and make sure there's nothing else in there before I stitch you up." She used a little microscope connected to a TV on the wall so everyone could see.

"Do you want to see the piece?" she asked.

"Only if it's really big!" I replied.

That comment had everyone laughing.

The surgeon showed me what could have been a tiny sliver of the nail on my pinky finger. It was indeed a piece of Pampered Chef stoneware.

Just kill me now.

She then leaned close to my ear. "You can tell your husband it was really big. Your secret is safe with me."

Seriously. Could this get any worse or more embarrassing? Well, yes. Yes, it could. And it did.

Once they were done stitching and bandaging me up, the nurse wheeled me back to the changing room. On the way there, several of the nurses stopped us.

"Is this the Pampered Chef stoneware girl?" each would ask. "I didn't know that stoneware could break so easily. After all, I've had my [insert their favorite stoneware item here] for years!"

My face was bright red by the time I got to my room. I dressed as quickly as I could, then sat back in my chair and waited for Kevin. I was absolutely dreading his arrival and the smartass look he'd likely give me.

There was a knock on the door, and Kevin appeared. Sure enough, he broke out a big ol' grin as he took in the sight of me and my overly bandaged foot.

The first words out of his mouth were, "Oh my gosh— they did all this for that tiny sliver in your ankle?"

I promptly corrected him. "Actually, it wasn't tiny. It was a large piece of stoneware!" But then I burst out laughing.

Living with the Lid Up
Lesson
∾

Sometimes objects in the mirror are larger than they appear. Sometimes little things drive us nuts or cause us great worry.

For matters big or small, I have found that it's much easier to face them head-on versus letting them simmer or stew. If you don't take action right away, even a small issue can eat at you or consume your thoughts, leaving you with coulda, shoulda, and woulda. Ain't nobody got time for those three stooges!

I think this is especially true when it comes to our health and relationships. In particular, we women tend to put our own needs last, after the needs of our husbands, kids, dogs, hermit crabs (oh wait—those died a few years ago), and jobs. Even when we secretly worry about our health symptoms, we outwardly downplay them as "probably nothing." Maybe that's because we're afraid of sounding like hypochondriacs, because we feel we don't have time to go to the doctor, or because we don't want to shell out for copays and deductibles.

For men, there's often an unstated pressure to "man up," "tough it out," or otherwise ignore and deny health issues. I know one man who said, "If I never go to the doctor, I'll never get cancer."

Why do we do this to ourselves? Instead, we need to listen to our intuition and take health issues seriously. That's true for women *and* men.

I followed my intuition in the case of the stoneware sliver. Yes, it turned out to be only a tiny piece. And yes, the whole experience was embarrassing. But still, I'm glad I followed through with it rather than ignored it and let it create pain and possible complications down the road.

And here's another—more serious—example from about five years ago. For a week or so, I was having some strange symptoms in my pelvic region. One night while watching TV, I started thinking I should consult Dr. Google about the symptoms.

All of a sudden, I heard the news anchor say something about ovarian cancer. Immediately, I tuned in, glued to the TV, as they showed a segment on ovarian cancer, its symptoms, and how dangerous it is.

I don't know if it was the synchronicity or what, but it freaked me out. The next morning, I booked an appointment with my ob-gyn.

Kevin was supportive, yet he couldn't help but ask, "Are you sure you want to go in? You've only had symptoms for a week."

"What if it's cancer?" I responded simply. "What if I wait and it progresses? What if it could mean the difference between life and death?"

Now, that might seem a little overdramatic. But was it? How many people with cancer or other terminal diseases can say they noticed symptoms long before they went in for a checkup?

I decided that my sanity and my health were worth the $150 to $200 the appointment would likely cost. Thankfully, everything turned out okay—no cancer, no illness—nothing except a ton of relief.

Whether we're talking stoneware splinters or cancer, I challenge you all to tune in to your intuition and trust your gut when it comes to health issues. After all, I don't think it could ever steer you wrong.

Chapter 14

The Purse I Lived to Tell About

I could hardly contain myself—my mom had just invited me on a girls' trip to New York with her and her friends. I was really excited to go to the Big Apple for the first time. But honestly, I was excited by the mere prospect of being able to use the bathroom without any interruptions. After all, I had two little boys at home. I rarely had five minutes to myself, let alone five whole days. If you have kids, you know what I'm talking about.

We girls had a long list of places and things we wanted to see. In the first four days, we saw two Broadway plays; visited the Statue of Liberty, then took a sunset cruise; went to the top of the Empire State Building; toured Wall Street; and visited the 9/11 Memorial, which was incredibly moving and emotional. Throughout all this, we tried new foods and visited every pub we could find. We were having an amazing vacation.

But for some reason, we felt something was missing. It wasn't until we visited Chinatown and Little Italy that our trip became complete.

You see, one of the things we found invigorating was all the people selling counterfeit purses and wallets illegally on the streets. You would be walking down a busy sidewalk, and someone would whisper in your ear, "Gucci, Kate Spade, Louis Vuitton . . . ?" Then they would watch you carefully. If you showed signs of interest, they'd suddenly open the garbage bag you didn't even know they were holding. Right before your eyes, several knockoff purses would appear, ready for you to buy.

I don't know why I found this so exhilarating. What makes it even funnier is I've never really considered myself a purse person, and I definitely never cared about designer labels. Yet something about buying counterfeit purses on the streets of Chinatown thrilled me to no end. Apparently, this suburban wife and mother of two young boys had been jonesing for some illegal activity in her life.

After our first illegal purse-buying adventure, we were eager to up the ante. While we were shopping in a little store on the edge of Chinatown, a woman approached us.

"Versace, Givenchy?"

We gave her the universal nod.

The woman led us through a tiny door in the back of the store. The little room we entered was literally six feet square, and there were eight of us in there. Tons of knockoff designer purses lined the walls. Needless to say, I bought one. That was the second—or maybe even third—purse for the girl who didn't care about purses.

Just as we were about to leave, a voice came over the lady's walkie-talkie—the police were in the store, just outside this secret little room. She motioned for us to be super quiet. Did I mention it was ninety-five degrees and humid that day? We could barely breathe.

After a few tense minutes, she finally told us we were okay to leave. Back out on the street, all we could say was, "That was *so* cool!"

Our shopping adventures continued as we strolled through the streets of Little Italy. A short young Hispanic man approached us. "Gucci, Givenchy, Coach?"

Once again, we gave the universal nod. Off we went on our purse-buying crime spree.

We followed our "guide" through an alley, then another alley, then he stopped just outside an apartment building. I looked back at my mom and her friends and raised my eyebrows.

"Think we should do this?" I asked quietly.

At that moment, I also thought about Kevin's wise words before I left: "Use your head and don't do anything stupid."

Hmm . . . this probably qualified as stupid. And yet, I wasn't too worried. Giving this short little guy another look, I knew I could take him if need be.

So inside the building we went. As we made our way up several flights of stairs, I inconspicuously took pictures with my phone—in case the police needed clues to solve my murder.

Finally, we reached a door. Our guide knocked three times. The door opened, and another gentleman appeared.

Oh shit . . . maybe this wasn't a good idea after all, I thought.

I was torn. Despite how dangerous the situation seemed, I still wasn't too worried. All I could think was, *What if the most amazing purses are through this doorway? Is this a risk worth taking?* Decisions, decisions.

For some reason, my feet took over. I strutted right into the apartment, cocky as could be. The other ladies followed my lead.

It was a dreary-looking apartment. I glanced around and saw two other men, bringing the total to four. I'll admit the sight made my cockiness dissipate a bit, yet I still believed we'd be okay.

That said, I did start searching for escape routes while simultaneously imagining my own funeral. (I'm relatively good at multitasking.) Just as my best friend, Jenny, was finishing up her heartfelt eulogy in my head, one of the gentlemen opened another door.

Suddenly, there it was—as if the gates of heaven had opened with the angels singing that golden, harmonic "Aaaaaaahhhhh!"

This room was *spectacular*. It was lit with several beautiful crystal chandeliers. The floors were a sparkly white marble. And all around the room were shelves with the most amazing knockoff designer purses showcased with little lights. It looked like a designer showroom, and each purse was calling our names.

We were awestruck—and honestly, quite thankful we were still alive. Our risk had paid off.

After our experience shopping in this amazing secret apartment boutique, we knew there was no way we could top it. Thus, we ended our purse-buying crime spree.

I left New York with five new purses I didn't even know I wanted and a story I would never share with my husband.

Well, until now, I suppose—when he reads this chapter.

Living with the Lid Up
Lesson
∾

In business and in life, we are constantly faced with risk. Do we move our family cross-country to live in a tiny home? Do we add a new product or service offering to our business? Do we homeschool our kids or put them in private school?

Risks and rewards are all around us. How do you tell which risk will be worth taking? This may sound cliché, but I've found it's always important to go with your gut instinct.

On paper, I *know* my story about buying purses in New York sounds dangerous. And I *know* we shouldn't have followed a strange man into an apartment building, let alone walked into an apartment where three other strange men were waiting. But in the moment, my gut told me there was no actual danger. And it was right.

That doesn't mean, though, that I simply turned off my brain. I relied on my common sense to validate what my gut was telling me: I knew we were secure with our strength in numbers, I knew I could fend off our guide, and I knew I had to stay one step ahead with contingency plans.

But your gut feeling only pays off if you listen to it. That's especially true in business. I once brought on a new client, even though I had a gut feeling she'd be a PITA.

But she seems really nice, I somehow convinced myself. *Don't worry—she won't be a PITA.*

Alas, that's exactly what she ended up being. You can guess how the story ended. I totally regretted the decision, yet I had no one to blame but myself.

Listen to your gut—it'll never steer you wrong. That goes for purses, PITAs, and most anything else.

Chapter 15

The Big Fat Nasty

୰

L et me start by saying I'm deathly afraid of snakes and have been since I was eleven. I developed this healthy fear when my parents took my brother and me to Reptile Gardens in South Dakota.

My brother and I were checking out this humongous python in a cage. The plaque near the cage featured the story of how this python had bitten the arm of the man who captured it. The pictures were pretty horrific.

I think I can speak for both of us—we were scared. (Gulp!)

Behind us, our mom said, "Smile!"

We turned toward her to smile at the camera. When the flash went off, though, the snake lunged, and its cage moved. Oh my God! To this day, I can still picture that snake and remember my fear when the entire caged moved. Again, I can speak for the both of us about that shared experience, so I know it left my brother with a healthy fear of snakes as well.

That fear is alive and well today too. I'm convinced we have a snake pit under our front porch. Those slithery creatures are everywhere. My snake-dar (snake radar) is always on.

In fact, several of our family members, friends, and neighbors have seen my Air Jordan maneuver when a snake goes near my foot. I can jump and climb through the air within seconds. People have also seen me convulse involuntarily, like someone having a seizure, when one of those nasty little serpents jumps out between the sidewalk and front step.

But of all the snakes plaguing me in my own yard, the Big Fat Nasty is the worst. It is a three-foot-long garter snake that has terrified us—and several of our lawn-maintenance guys— over the seventeen years we've lived in our home. For the past ten of those years, we've made many attempts to capture it, yet somehow the Big Fat Nasty remains at large.

One day when the boys and I were coming home, I parked in the driveway, then opened the garage door so we could use the access door to get inside the house. We were about to walk in the garage, when we heard ssssomething. We must have been quite a sight as we froze right where the concrete meets the pavement. We leaned in to listen to the ssssound of ssssomething ssssslithering. It came from the top of the open garage door.

I gave Max and Sam a perplexed look. "That can't be a snake, can it?"

After all, how in the world could a snake get on top of the garage door, especially since we had just opened it? We stood there for a few more moments, and then we heard it again.

Max scratched his chin. "It must just be the wind," he claimed.

I was not convinced.

So, I did what any loving mother would do and told the boys to run into the garage, head inside the house, and go around to unlock the front door for me. Before you start judging me, remember what they say when you're on a plane: you should put your oxygen mask on first, before you help your child with his. I'm quite certain this rule translates to "Parents, save yourself first," and it applies to snake situations as well.

My boys begrudgingly did as they were told and let their loving mommy in the front door. Once I was inside, I breathed a sigh of relief.

As I started putting away my things, Max announced he was heading outside to play with the neighbor kids. But less than a minute later, he came bolting back into the kitchen, screaming with a terrified look on his face.

I grabbed him. "What? What's the matter?"

He looked at me with big eyes and a quivering jaw. "It was the Big Fat Nasty!"

I gasped and covered my mouth.

As he explained what had happened, I played out the indisputable near-death experience in my head. You see, the ssssound we heard was indeed the Notorious BFN on top of the garage door. (I'm still not sure how that happened, and I don't want to spend one more minute thinking about it either.) When Max went out through the garage to join his friends, the Big Fat Nasty fell off the garage door and landed right next to Max before slithering away.

Seriously, if that thing had landed on my shoulder, I would have died of an instant heart attack. My husband would be widowed, and my two boys would be without their loving mother. Can you imagine reading that obituary?

Living with the Lid Up
Lesson
ᵔᵔ

We all have things we fear in life. However, it's important not to let the fear take over your life and consume you. Instead, you need to recognize the fear, understand where it stems from, and own it or address it.

Me, I certainly recognize my fear of snakes, I certainly know where it comes from, and I certainly own it. (By the way, many have tried to talk me into confronting my fear through some form of immersion therapy. However, I have *no* plans of doing that—ever!)

I may be afraid of snakes, but I don't let it consume me. If I did, I would pack up my family and all my belongings and move to either Antarctica, Greenland, Hawaii, Iceland, Ireland or New Zealand—places where there are no snakes. (Don't believe me? Just google it.) Instead, I go about my life as best as I can, knowing at any moment I may need to leap over a reptile, or I may need to duck as one somehow falls from the garage door.

In business, many of us actually have the same fears, such as the fear of failure. This is especially true for those of us who took that leap of faith and started our own businesses. But we can't let fear of failure paralyze us and keep us from doing great things. And we can't hide it or keep it under lock and key either.

Instead, we need to recognize our fear for what it is and embrace it together. I find it extremely helpful and therapeutic to share my fears with my peers. I know they're likely experiencing some version of the same fear, or maybe they've overcome that fear and can offer ideas or advice.

This happened recently at a conference in Santa Barbara. In our free time, one of my favorite clients and I went for a walk along the beach. As we strolled, watching the ocean, we talked about our fears regarding business growth and financials. My client's company has been in existence way longer than mine and is considerably larger, yet she too shared the same fears. I took great comfort in knowing I wasn't alone. We formed a bond because we allowed ourselves to be vulnerable and to share our fears openly and honestly.

My friend, you are not alone either. Don't let your fears consume you. Find a friend or a peer who will listen and help as you share your thoughts and fears openly and honestly. I guarantee you will feel lighter and freer when you do.

Chapter 16

Red Heels + Pickles + Leather = Disaster

Have you ever overbooked or overcommitted yourself? It's not a fun feeling, is it? I think this especially happens to women because we try to do it all and never want to let anyone down.

Case in point, what do you say when your child begs you to be a chaperone on a field trip, you have a packed work schedule, you have to take the dogs to the vet, you have to bake cookies for the church picnic, and you know it's virtually impossible to do it all? I bet you say, "Sure, honey. I'll be a chaperone." But then you spend the next several minutes berating your inability to say no, all the while running multiple calculations to figure out how you can make the impossible possible.

Sound familiar? I do it all the time. Just when I think I'm getting better at saying no and trying not to pretend I'm Wonder Woman, I relapse and say yes.

A great example was when I knowingly—again, *knowingly*—booked two back-to-back ninety-minute workshops plus a webinar with 250 people on the same day. Brilliant . . . right?

Well, even when I know I don't need to be Wonder Woman, it's still amazing what I can do when I'm under the gun. I don't know how I did it, but I pulled it off with little to no sleep. Both of my workshops were a hit, and I rocked my webinar, if I do say so myself. I think it helped that I wore my sweet red heels.

Of course, I was completely exhausted when I was done, but I couldn't head home right away. I had a mess to clean up. We had provided breakfast for the morning workshop and lunch for the second workshop. Thanks to Kevin's natural inclinations when ordering food, we had about three times too much, leaving us with a ton of leftovers. (Love you, honey.)

In particular, I didn't want all those untouched Jimmy John's sandwiches to go to waste. I did a quick fist pump once I realized the leftover food was actually a blessing in disguise. Now I wouldn't need to cook dinner. I could proceed straight to my bathtub and my chardonnay.

As I was packing up the sandwiches for the boys, I noticed a container of Jimmy John's pickles. It was opened, but no one had eaten any. Our family has a slight pickle addiction, so I had to bring them home too.

I searched and searched for the lid, but alas, it was not to be found. However, I wasn't willing to give up and let those tasty green treats go to waste. I covered the container with a plastic bag and hoped it wouldn't spill in the brand-new car I'd had for only a week.

You don't need to be a psychic to see where this story is going.

After packing up the food and strategically placing it in my back seat, I began my journey at last. I couldn't wait to trade my sweet red heels (that were not-so-sweetly causing my feet to throb) for a nice warm bubble bath and glass of wine. Sounds magnificent, doesn't it?

On my way, Kevin called to find out how the events had gone. I told him everything had been a smashing success—but I also told him to *never ever* let me book more than one event on the same day again.

He just laughed. We both knew it was pretty much inevitable. I've been wired like this my whole life. It's hard to drop the Wonder Woman cape sometimes.

Just then, on the final turn into our neighborhood, something toppled over in the back seat. It was the pickles. I screamed, hung up, and immediately pulled over.

Side note: It's not a great idea to scream into the phone while driving and then hang up on your significant other. Apparently, it can cause a little stress and anxiety.

I opened my car door, jumped out in those sweet red heels, flung open the back door, righted the container of pickles, and still managed to answer my phone as my frantic husband tried to reach me.

"It's the pickles—I'll call you back!" I shouted before hanging up again.

Pickle juice was just floating there on top of the leather seats, and I had nothing to clean it up with. With the car being only a week old, I hadn't even been through a drive-through yet to stock up on napkins for the glove compartment.

All I could do was use my hand to cup the pickle juice and dump it into another container. What a mess! It was the best I could do until I got home and properly cleaned it. So much for my bubble bath and chardonnay.

I shut the back door and headed for the driver's seat when I noticed something: the car was making a strange beeping sound. It wasn't until I shut my door and tried to put my car in drive that I realized why it was beeping. In my panic to fix the pickle situation, I had left my car in gear.

Fortunately, but unbeknownst to me, my vehicle has an automatic emergency-brake safety feature for exhausted business owners in red heels who pull over and forget to put their car in park while cleaning up pickle juice in the back seat.

Instantly, I imagined how different this story could have played out. I envisioned newspaper and TV headlines: "Entrepreneur in Red Heels Run over by Own Car While Holding Jar of Pickles" or "Businesswoman Carries Jar of Pickles While Chasing Her Car down Hill in Red Heels—Live Video at Ten!"

Living with the Lid Up

Lesson

∽

Yes, we can tap into Wonder Woman (or Superman) powers from time to time in order to make the impossible possible. But it's important to avoid using those powers *all* the time. We are mere humans. Acting as if we're indestructible, perfect superheroes when it comes to juggling work and life will likely result in burnout, screwups, or much worse.

So stop saying yes to every request. Think of it this way: for every yes you give, you ultimately say no to something else.

Here are a couple of other key lessons I learned from this experience:

1. It's important to schedule your time wisely and abide by the scheduling systems you put in place. Believe it or not, I do have a scheduling system that saves me from my own overbooking tendencies. I override it only when there's a great business opportunity I can't pass up. The trick is to leave enough margin in your schedule and life so you're ready to take on those superhuman feats from time to time.

2. Sometimes when we move too fast, we make *big* mistakes. Have you ever been in a rush to send out an email campaign and forgotten to check if your links worked or if it was mobile responsive? It's important to slow down. And you usually can't slow down if

you're trying to squeeze too many commitments into a single day or week.

3. Find humility in all you do. I'll say it yet again: We are human, and we make mistakes. (Some of which make for funny stories, great blog topics, and insightful lessons.)

4. And last but certainly not least, pickles and new leather are not a great combination. I had to air out my car for over two weeks before the smell began to fade.

Chapter 17

Cabbage Patch Christmas

∿

It all began on Christmas morning, 1987.

By tradition, my family exchanged presents on Christmas Eve, and then we'd wake up on Christmas morning to find what Santa had left in our stockings. He'd bring us all kinds of goodies and usually one big toy as well.

I woke before anyone else that morning. (I've always been a morning person, and Christmas morning was no exception.) I sprung out of bed and ran out of my room. I was so excited I could hardly contain myself.

That year, I had been pining for another Cabbage Patch Kids doll. I had several already but was always interested in more. I assumed, of course, that Santa had come through on his end of the bargain. I couldn't wait to see the new Cabbage Patch Kid that would be sitting under my stocking.

But to my horror, there wasn't a Cabbage Patch Kid under my stocking; instead, there was one under my four-year-old brother's stocking.

Ugh!

Why didn't Santa bring *me* the doll? Didn't he read my letter? "CABBAGE PATCH KID" was at the top of my list in big bold print. And seeing that doll under my brother's stocking, not mine, made me covet it even more. What was my dumb brother going to do with a doll anyway?

That's when a devious plan began to form in my brain. What if I simply put the doll under *my* stocking? Who would be the wiser? My parents surely wouldn't know. They would never realize Santa had left it for Brent and not me.

Then again, I saw the doll was named Rufus Brent. Maybe Santa did bring it for him because of the name. I couldn't take his present, could I?

I wrestled with the little devil resting on one shoulder and the little angel on the other. But I eventually decided Santa must have had a reason to give my brother the doll. I didn't want to tempt fate or risk the chance of getting coal in my stocking next Christmas.

So, I left the doll under my brother's stocking and went back to opening the items in my own stocking. To this day, I have no idea what I got. All I know is that it wasn't a Cabbage Patch Kid!

Living with the Lid Up
Lesson
∽

You're probably thinking, *Well, the lesson of this story is pretty easy: you shouldn't steal your brother's presents.*

Yes, that is a good lesson. But assuming you're not an eight-year-old, it's not really applicable to your life.

So what are you *really* supposed to take away from this short-but-sweet chapter? It's that holidays are a gold mine for stories that help us connect. Even if we celebrate different holidays, there's something universal about them that brings us together.

I bet my story struck a chord with you. For example, did you have—or want—Cabbage Patch Kids? Were you envious of your sibling's presents or ever come close to secretly swapping stocking stuffers? Did you ever wrestle with how to handle disappointment over a gift?

Now that I've shared this story with you, you may realize we have something in common—a great starting point for building a relationship.

So dip into your holiday treasure trove of stories when engaging with clients, prospects, coworkers, and especially family and friends. I promise it'll help you cultivate deeper, more meaningful relationships.

Chapter 18

The Bubble Gum Blunder

∿

"The Bubble Gum Blunder" sounds like an intriguing title, right? Well, it's actually quite a funny story—though it wasn't really funny when it happened.

Several years ago, I was the marketing director at an accounting firm. We were super excited about a new partnership we'd formed with a national franchise. We had a special opportunity to pitch a fixed-price accounting and payroll package to their five-hundred-plus franchisees across the country. It would be a huge promotional campaign. Our goal was to not only promote the franchise partnership but also show that our accounting firm was "fun" so we could hopefully convert the individual franchisees into customers.

But let's face it: no one really wants to hear from an accounting firm. We knew we had to be übercreative. After hours of strategizing, we came up with a really cool multimedia outreach campaign with five components. (Side note: I might be a bit biased, as I created it.)

Here's a little snapshot of what we sent with each step of the campaign.

- Step 1: a personalized letter from the owner of the accounting firm with an overview of the program and a testimonial from the national franchisee director
- Step 2: a stress ball along with a note card that reads, "Do taxes stress you out?"
- Step 3: a personalized email from me with our current newsletter attached and a link to join our list to get lots of great tips on avoiding IRS penalties.
- Step 4: an educational flyer titled "Top 5 Mistakes Most Small Businesses Make When It Comes to Their Accounting/Bookkeeping/Taxes" along with a package of bubble gum and a Post-it note that said, "Something to Chew On . . . "
- Step 5: a call from me to more formally introduce our firm and see if they were interested in a complimentary assessment of their financial picture

Pretty cool, right?

We kicked off the campaign, and things were moving along wonderfully. After completing step 4 with the flyer, gum, and Post-it note, I geared myself up for step 5: making five hundred semi-cold calls. (Yep, it sounds like as much fun as banging your head against the wall. Unless, of course, you're one of those weird people who like to cold-call. Ick!)

But then something unexpected happened. I got a call from the post office regarding the mailing for step 4 I had just dropped off. Apparently, each piece was short postage—it was overweight because of the bubble gum, even though our internal postage machine hadn't indicated that. The post office said the mailing went out, but each piece had been marked "Postage due upon delivery."

My heart sank. I instantly started sweating. In a promotional campaign with five hundred franchisees we hoped to turn into customers, I had just forced them all to pay postage for our mailing. Definitely not "fun."

What in the world could I do? My mind raced with both rational and totally irrational options. *Should I turn in my resignation because I'm such a doughhead? Or should I simply hide under my desk and forget the whole thing happened? Should I say anything to my boss? What if one of the franchisees calls and my boss finds out what happened? Should I tell him the story and blame it on this issue between our post office and our postage machine?*

After I collected myself (and picked myself up off the floor), I realized I needed to find the humor in this situation. *Maybe, just maybe, I can redeem myself if I do something clever to turn this situation around.*

The very next day, I told my boss the whole story and my plan to fix it. I then promptly asked for a check for $500. I took the check, drove right to the bank, and got five hundred crisp one-dollar bills.

Next, I found a clever and funny comic about postage mistakes. I picked one that wasn't offensive, though, in case the franchisees happened to personally know postal employees. I incorporated the comic into a letter apologizing and explaining the situation. I added a one-dollar bill to each letter, sent off the mailing (after verifying the postage amount a hundred times), crossed my fingers, and said a bazillion prayers.

Guess what happened? I got a *ton* of calls and emails from the franchisees upon receiving my "so sorry" mailing. Each one of them remarked on how impressed they were that I came forward, explained the situation, and compensated them for the postage—all in a creative way.

Being honest and vulnerable about the blunder helped me build rapport and trust with these prospective clients. Who wouldn't want to work with an accounting firm that was trustworthy, honest, and fun?

When you really look at it, we gained new customers because of—not in spite of—this bubble gum blunder. More importantly, this blunder gave us an unexpected opportunity to make a positive impression and statement about our credibility.

Living with the Lid Up

Lesson

As we've discussed in several chapters now, mistakes happen. After all, we're all human, right? It's what you do next that really matters.

I could have easily pretended this blunder hadn't happened, while I hoped and prayed nobody found out. But because my integrity and reputation are important to me, I chose instead to go the honorable route, fess up, and fix it.

Has something such as this ever happened to you? Maybe you screwed up on a project with a client or miscalculated the numbers you gave to your boss. What did you do next?

If you handled your past blunders with integrity, good for you. If not . . . it's never too late to turn a new leaf. Start thinking now about what you can do if (or when) you find yourself in a blunder down the road.

Chapter 19

Did I Just Poop on the Table?

∿

When you're pregnant, there are so many things people do not tell you about labor and delivery. I'm guessing this is by design. If expectant mothers heard all the gory details of childbirth, we'd never want to conceive, right?

After my experience giving birth to my first child, I made it my life's mission to educate and inform my friends about what actually happens in the delivery room. I simply tell them to call me whenever they're ready. I'll bring a bottle of wine (for me, of course, not them) and fill them in on everything they need to know. Many of my friends have told me afterward how thankful they were that I clued them in before they gave birth.

So, my friends, please consider this chapter part of that mission to tell it like it is when it comes to labor and delivery. Even if you have no plans of ever giving birth or witnessing one, come along for the ride, will you? I promise there's a larger lesson at the end.

For me, one of the scariest parts of my first pregnancy was the childbirth class, which we took about three months before my due date. For many expectant moms, childbirth class is a rude awakening. Up to that point, pregnancy has been mostly fun and exciting as you look forward to your new little bundle of joy. But the childbirth class suddenly forces you to face the stark reality: your little bundle has to pop out of you, and all sorts of stuff will happen while you do it.

Kevin and I decided to do one full-weekend class versus several weekly classes. So naturally, my husband had the great idea to go out with his buddy Friday night and tie one on so he would be incredibly hung over for our class at nine o'clock Saturday morning. It was pretty entertaining to watch him turn three shades of green during the "miracle of birth" video. It took everything I had not to bust out laughing.

Then the next video started playing, and karma decided to bite me in the butt. If you've taken a childbirth class in the past fifteen to twenty years, you likely saw the same video. The images still haunt me; I can recall them in a moment's notice. Let's see if you remember too.

A woman appears on screen. She looks to be in her early forties, and she resembles Farrah Fawcett. She is in the hospital with absolutely no clothes on. She claims how free she feels with her whole body exposed for everyone to see through the entire labor.

Mortified, I was now three shades of green too. Once the movie was done, I leaned over and whispered in Kevin's ear. "I get to wear a hospital gown at least, right?" I'm not sure why I asked him this question. This was his first time too. But I had to know.

All he could do was shrug.

I was so concerned that I called my mother during the break and asked her this question. She reassured me I could wear a gown if I wanted. Whew—what a relief! The whole naked-as-a-jaybird thing was a deal breaker for me.

As the day progressed and Kevin's hangover started to wane, we continued to learn more and more about the baby and what life would be like after we brought our little one home. I started to regain my confidence and had almost blocked Farrah's twin from my mind.

But then they played one last video. Just when I thought things were looking up, I found out that sometimes women get episiotomies. (Make sure you're sitting down if you have to google that term. On second thought—no, *don't* google it. Just wait until I can come over with that bottle of wine, and we'll talk.)

As if episiotomies weren't bad enough, the video also said that sometimes women poop on the table when they start pushing.

Oh, hell no! That will not be me. There is no way I will embarrass myself like that. Nope. Not happening.

From that moment forward, my nightly prayers consisted of "Please give us a healthy baby" and "Lord, please don't let me poop on the table."

Fast-forward to the big day, my due date. Guess what? Nothing happened, despite trying all the little-known tricks I could google to induce labor. Apparently, the little guy wasn't ready quite yet.

Contractions started the day after my due date, though. I spent all day timing them. When they were two to three minutes apart, I alerted Kevin. Off we went to the hospital.

This was it! I was excited and terrified. On the way to the hospital, I may or may not have said an extra prayer for a healthy baby and no poop on the table.

We got all checked in, and the contractions kept pounding me. They were really bad, as it turned out, because it was back labor. Anyone who's lived through back labor knows it ain't fun to have the back of a human skull scraping and sliding down your sacrum.

But after several tests, a nurse gave me a condescending look. "Honey, your contractions aren't strong enough," she snapped. "We're going to send you home. Hopefully you'll be back in a couple of days."

I have never been a violent person. But within thirty seconds, I envisioned all the ways I wanted to strangle this nurse. Don't you just love how labor can take a sane, sweet, calm woman and turn her into a raging she-devil?

Because I would apparently be dealing with these intense contractions for the next couple of days on my own, the nurse gave me some pain medication and told me to eat something with them.

(By the way, this nurse was the only bad one I had. All the other nurses were nothing short of amazing—besides the nipple Nazi. But we won't go there).

After the nurse left the room, I looked at Kevin. "If I have to go through this much pain, there's no way I can do this. They'll have to find another way to get this baby out of me, because this ain't happening."

We got back in the car and headed home. I felt crushed.

The last thing I wanted to do was eat, but Kevin, the rule follower, knew I needed it for the pain medication. He stopped at McDonald's and ordered a number 1 for himself and a strawberry sundae for me. (They are the bomb, aren't they? I think I consumed about five hundred of them during that pregnancy alone.)

After we got home and ate, Kevin went to move all our stuff from my tiny Jetta to our conversion van. (Yep, there's another story there too.) While he was in the garage, I lay on our living room floor with Shelby, Jake, and Randy—our three beagles—watching me.

All of a sudden, I had a massive contraction. As I got on my hands and knees to stretch my back, I threw up strawberry sundae all over our white carpeting. As if that weren't bad enough, when I shifted my body weight again, my water broke all over our carpet too.

I'll never forget the look I got from the beagles. With cocked heads, they stared at me in disbelief, like, *What is she doing?*

Two to three days, my ass! It was go time!

My pants were wrecked, so I stripped off everything below the waist. Then I yelled for Kevin and pounded on the wall.

He came flying in and took one look at me and the carpet. "What in the hell happened? I was gone for only three minutes!"

"The baby's coming!" I told him. "Go grab me a towel so I can wrap it around my waist."

After all that fretting about nakedness, I was ready and willing to go to the hospital wearing only a shirt and a towel.

Isn't it funny how the one thing you dread the most doesn't seem to be a big deal in the moment?

Kevin, however, wasn't so willing. "There is no way you're going half-naked!"

I begrudgingly put on some clothes.

It hadn't even been an hour since our discharge, yet we were heading back to the hospital. Along the way, Kevin got a new decoration on his armrest in the van—I bit into it during a contraction. And when he stopped at a red light, I told him in a deep, demonic voice, "JUUUST RUUUN IIIIT!" He later told me he thought I was possessed.

Kevin left the van parked at the curb outside the emergency entrance while he ran in to grab a wheelchair. As he wheeled me down the hallway, I tapped my wrists, getting them ready for the IV that would come with the epidural. (I have to tell you, I'm a baby when it comes to pain.)

As we rounded the corner, a woman came down the hall. Kevin was so embarrassed as I yelled "WWWAAATCH OOOUUUT!" in that deep, demonic voice.

We finally made it to the labor and delivery floor. They checked me in and gave me a ton of drugs. I had made it in time to get my epidural to take the edge off the back labor. Finally, things were starting to look up.

However, it was getting pretty late at night, and my contractions started to level off. The staff told me to get some sleep. (Yeah, right.) If my contractions didn't pick back up by morning, they'd give me Pitocin to kick-start them.

In hindsight, I should have told them to just make it happen. How can you sleep when it feels like a torpedo is going to shoot out your ass?

Morning came, and the contractions were still the same. They gave me some Pitocin, Bada bing, bada boom—within a few hours, that little guy was ready and raring to come out. It was time to push. Thank God!

I tried to remember the childbirth class and how we should breathe during delivery, but nothing came to me. So I just pushed as hard as I could. Nothing. I pushed again. Nothing. Then I gave her all I had. At last, there was some relief—and a strange smell.

I should have known by the look on Kevin's face, but I asked anyway. In the middle of major contractions, I looked up at him and asked, "Did I just poop on the table?"

He looked at me with hesitation, uncertain of whether to tell me the truth. Then, with his eyes downcast, he nodded his head, probably terrified of my response. After all, I'd been praying for three months that this wouldn't happen.

Instead, I surprised him by saying, "Wow, that felt amazing!"

Yes, that's right, folks: I pooped on the table and was proud of it! That is one phrase I never thought would come out of my mouth, let alone one I would write in a book for all to read.

After several more pushes and an episiotomy, Max was born at 12:17 p.m. on July 17, 2003, weighing in at eight pounds, eight ounces and measuring twenty-two inches long.

Living with the Lid Up

Lesson
∿

Have you ever gotten yourself so worked up about something, letting it consume your thoughts, only to discover it was no big deal in the end?

Don't sweat the small stuff.

Those of you who've given or witnessed birth probably already know this. I bet you read this chapter with a little smile, knowing that all those fears about nakedness and, yes, even poop would turn out to be only passing fears when the real moment arrived.

For those of you who will someday experience birth for the first time, please just keep this story in mind. I'm sure you too will freak out a bit as you learn about the things that can or will happen as you bring your bundle of joy into the world. But when that time comes, hopefully you'll be better able to shrug off the small stuff.

But as promised, this story is about more than just birth. Poop aside, there are real lessons here that anyone can apply to business.

For example, maybe you need to have a conversation with your client about scope creep, which is when a project's cost and scope grows in unpredictable ways after you get started. For days, you worry about how to explain why you'll have to increase prices. You prepare this lengthy explanation, worrying you'll lose the client or, at the very least, end up with a tense exchange.

But when the time comes for the conversation, your client simply says, "OK, sounds good!" after your first sentence.

Think about all the time, all the energy you wasted worrying when it turned out to be no big deal. Sound familiar?

Try this instead: when you're worried about something, pray or meditate on it, then move on and let it play out on its own. I know it's easier said than done. If you need help, think about a situation where you wasted time and energy worrying needlessly. It might help you move on quicker.

(And if all else fails, ask yourself, "Did I just poop on the table?" That should do the trick!)

Chapter 20

June 2, 2018

ᘒ

All in all, it was a pretty normal day.

Until it wasn't.

When I woke up that morning, I looked out the window of our cabin. *Ugh!* I thought. *It's raining, and it's only forty-five degrees. But isn't it June?*

Apparently, Mother Nature wasn't aware that my boys had only half a week of school left, and then it'd officially be summer in Minnesota.

Still, we decided to make the most of the day. Even though it was cold and rainy, we could at least go four-wheeling. We loved getting out to enjoy nature in our side-by-sides, which are two-person ATVs.

So we packed a cooler of beverages and snacks and dressed in layers. We were ready for our big ATV adventure. We would be heading about twenty miles north, where Kevin's cousin Greg had a cabin. Greg was excited to show us some new trails, and his brother Steve would be there too.

Before we left, I went back into our bedroom and had a rather strange thought. For some reason, I felt compelled to make our bed and pick up the room a bit, just in case someone had to come into our cabin. I'd never worried about that before, though. As strange as it seemed, I tidied up, then we headed out.

On our way up to Greg's place, the boys and I discussed all the things we wanted to do that summer. Max talked about biking to his friend Bryce's house every day to work on radio-controlled cars. Sam talked about hanging out with friends and paddleboarding.

Once we got to Greg's cabin, we prepped the ATVs and checked our gear. We were just about to leave when I remembered the bug spray I had left in the truck. When I ran to get it, I noticed several bandanas left over from our "Memorial Day Cowboy Cook-Out" theme party. I grabbed them as well as another blanket for the boys to sit on, as it was still raining a bit.

There were six of us—two in each of three side-by-sides. Greg and Steve took the lead, Kevin and I rode behind them, and our two boys brought up the rear. At fourteen, Max was driving.

To get to the ATV trail, we first had to take a shared road, which both ATVs and road vehicles could use. As we drove, we enjoyed the view of the trees with their bright-green leaves as well as the lakes that were no longer frozen. I remarked to Kevin how it was so cool that we were able to get out and enjoy nature, even though the weather was crappy.

We found our way to the ATV trail. After driving for about ten minutes, we decided to stop and check in with everyone. As the boys parked next to us, Max suddenly realized he didn't have his seat belt on. He quickly fastened it. Then he said his hands were a bit cold and asked to borrow Kevin's gloves, which Kevin graciously handed over. Max put them on and gave us a thumbs-up to indicate he was ready to ride.

Greg and Steve took off, and we and the boys followed behind, as usual. We headed down a shared road that led us to the next trail.

No more than a couple of minutes later, we rounded a corner and suddenly saw headlights. A truck was coming straight for us.

I can't even describe how surreal that moment was. My brain tried to register what was happening as we swerved into the ditch to avoid being hit head-on by the truck.

Seconds later, I heard a sound that will haunt me for the rest of my life—the crunch of metal on metal. The truck had hit our boys.

As I'd later come to understand, the driver of the truck tried to swerve away once he saw our ATVs. However, it was raining, his tires were bald, and he'd been drinking. It was a combination that almost proved deadly.

As the truck bore down on them, Max had only seconds to react. Thankfully, he managed to swerve just enough to avoid being hit head-on, which likely spared both his and his brother's lives in the process.

Kevin and I immediately leaped out of our ATV and raced to our boys. Just typing that gave me chills from head to toe. Sam was standing outside the ATV, which was crushed in the front-left corner. He was crying, but he appeared to be uninjured.

Unfortunately, we couldn't say the same about Max. He was still in the ATV, screaming and writhing in pain. His right leg was pinned in the wreck.

"Mom, Dad—help me! I'm stuck! I can't feel my legs!"

It's a phrase no parent ever wants to hear.

I think at that moment, God took over. He knew we would have to set aside our emotions. Instantly, we all took action to free Max from the ATV and get help as soon as possible.

As our party leapt into action, the driver of the truck and his two passengers jumped out. They were just kids—not much older than our boys, it seemed. They tried to figure out how they could help, but they also knew they had screwed up. The driver had been drinking.

We had to focus on Max, though. I immediately tried to call 911, but I couldn't get a cell signal. So Steve ran down the road a bit, caught a signal, and was able to call.

Meanwhile, Kevin and Greg hooked our ATV's winch cable to the boys' ATV in an attempt to pull the crushed portion off Max's leg. As they did that, I noticed smoke from the wreck was billowing in Max's face and getting trapped in his helmet, so I got inside the cab with him and removed the helmet. I looked down—there was so much blood pooling under his right foot. I knew the situation was bad. In hindsight, I'm glad I didn't know how dire it was at the time.

And then I noticed the bandanas. (Another God moment.) During the crash, the glove box had popped open, and the bandanas had spilled out. I grabbed a couple of bandanas, slipped them under his thigh, and tied a makeshift tourniquet on his right leg.

Max was still writhing in pain. I tried my best to calm him while praying for him at the same time.

With all the mud and rain, Kevin and Greg couldn't get enough traction to lift the boys' ATV using the winch on ours. So Greg and Kevin attached the boys' winch cable to the back of the driver's truck, and Greg hopped in. Thankfully, the truck had enough power and traction to lift the ATV.

The driver and his passengers helped me lift Max out. Greg and Kevin took the blanket I had grabbed from our truck before we left the cabin (obviously, God had a helping hand there too) and laid it on the road. We then laid Max on the blanket.

It was evident he had lost a lot of blood. He was starting to go into shock. Again, I'm glad I couldn't see the actual injury—hidden by his long pants—as I might have gone into shock too. We covered him with all our jackets and extra gear to warm him.

I knelt by him and stroked his forehead in an attempt to calm him—and myself. He was shaking and crying.

"Mom, I can't feel my legs! Mom, I think I'm paralyzed!" he cried.

"Max, take it easy, buddy," I said. "Everything is going to be okay."

I said those words to him, yet I was dying inside, praying with all I had that it really would be okay.

"In fact," I said, "why don't you try to wiggle your toes for me?"

Dear God, I silently prayed, *please don't let him be paralyzed.*

He looked up at me, then wiggled his toes.

"See, buddy? You're not paralyzed. You can move your toes, and that's a good thing! The ambulance is on the way," I added. "As soon as they get here, they'll help us."

Please, please, please let that ambulance get here soon.

With each minute, Max became more and more scared. He told Kevin and me that he loved us, and he said to tell Nana and Boppa and Grandma and Grandpa that he loved them too.

Another stab to my already bleeding heart—my little buddy believed he was going to die.

Finally, we heard the sound we'd been waiting to hear: the ambulance was near. From the time Steve had called 911, it had taken about fifteen to twenty minutes—an eternity—for help to arrive.

My moment of joy was short-lived, though, when I realized this ambulance unit consisted of community first responders. They were local volunteers who had some basic training in emergency response, but they were *not* paramedics. Apparently, this system is common in rural areas, but it was a new experience for me. We'd already waited so long for the ambulance to arrive, and all we wanted was for someone to take care of Max.

Bless their hearts—these women really wanted to help. But once they cut Max's pants and saw the state of the injury, they radioed that they needed to transport him to a Life Link helicopter at a nearby airport. From there, he would be flown to a Duluth hospital, as the local hospital couldn't handle this level of injury.

It was not a good sign at all. And not a good sight either. With Max's pants now cut, we had our first glimpse at the injury. Or at least Kevin did—he told me to look away. I'm glad I did.

A few moments later, more community first responders and some police officers arrived on the scene. They all worked together to get Max onto a stretcher and loaded into the back of the ambulance.

I jumped into the front seat of the ambulance while three first responders worked on making Max relatively comfortable in the back. Kevin, Sam, Steve, Greg, and the truck driver stayed behind to give their accounts to the police.

As we drove off with lights and sirens wailing, I yelled back to Max. "I'm here, buddy! Don't worry. We're going to get help."

I think he heard me. He began to calm slightly, despite being in great pain and obvious shock.

The ambulance driver, a sweet woman, explained that we were heading to the Ford Airport in Grand Rapids, where the medevac helicopter would be waiting to take Max to Duluth. Along the way, we'd meet up with another ambulance, this time with real paramedics.

Just then, Max yelled out in pain. The driver pushed the gas pedal a little bit harder.

Not knowing the extent of Max's injuries—other than they were bad enough to need a medevac—I decided we needed all the prayers we could get. So I sent a text to my parents, my brother, and my in-laws. I told them we'd been in an accident and that Max could use their prayers.

As I typed the message and hit send, tears started rolling down my cheeks. I was in shock. I couldn't get over what had just happened, how quickly life as we knew it had changed.

It always sounds so cliché when people say, "Live every day as if it's your last." However, that phrase is just a phrase until something such as this happens to you. Suddenly, you realize how truly precious life really is . . . especially when it's your child's life.

We continued to race up Highway 6, hoping we'd see the other ambulance soon. The first responders could only triage, not medicate. The real paramedics would be able to give Max something to help with the shock and pain.

Eventually, another ambulance with its lights on appeared in the distance, headed in our direction—a welcome sight. We pulled off the highway. Seconds later a paramedic joined the first responders in the back of our ambulance.

I let out a sigh of relief. Max would finally get something to curb the excruciating pain.

Later, he told me that whatever they gave him really messed him up. "Mom," he said, "it was so weird. After they gave me the shots, I started swearing and telling jokes—and I couldn't stop myself!"

I can only imagine what came out of his mouth. After all, I know his father and his father's sense of humor quite well.

Finally, we arrived at the airport. We drove onto the tarmac to meet the helicopter waiting for us.

"Will I be able to ride with Max in the helicopter?" I asked the driver.

"We'll have to check with the pilot," she replied. "They have weight restrictions."

Think skinny thoughts, Kari.

The pilot and paramedic opened the back doors of the ambulance and began unloading Max.

"Mom would like to ride with," the driver told the pilot. "Can she?"

I waited with bated breath for his answer. And this, my friends, is the only funny part about this story.

"That depends," the pilot said. "How much do you weigh, Mom?"

Oh my God! I'd been lying about my weight for at least twenty years. But now I had to tell the truth. Out loud. In front of seven total strangers.

All of them looked at me, waiting for my answer.

At last, I said the number. The pilot ran his calculations, then shook his head.

"Sorry—that won't work."

I was crushed. I was too fat to fly.

The crew finished unloading Max, then pushed him across the tarmac to the doors of the helicopter. I walked alongside the stretcher. I kissed my boy's forehead as the stretcher stopped.

"I love you," I told him. "We'll meet you at the Duluth hospital as soon as we can." I nodded toward the helicopter. "Hey, too bad it's not Chopper Dave," I said, referring to my cousin, who was a medevac pilot.

Max must have sensed I needed a little comic relief in that moment. "Yeah, where is that son of a bitch anyway?" he said with a slight slur.

Of course, my mom instincts kicked in. "Shh, Max—we don't talk like that." But even as I said it, a smile spread across my face.

Thanks for the little pick-me-up, buddy.

As I watched the helicopter fly away, I fought back tears. I knew I'd been holding it together for far too long. I just needed to find a place where I could come completely unglued.

Before I could do that, though, I had to call Kevin. We hadn't been in communication since Max and I had first left in the ambulance.

I reached Kevin and told him I was in the Life Link hangar at the Ford Airport, and that Max was on his way to St. Mary's Children's Hospital in Duluth.

"Wait a minute," he said. "You're not with Max? I thought you'd be flying with him."

"No. It turns out I'm too fat to fly!"

Kevin laughed hysterically, and I could hear Sam chuckling in the background too.

After Kevin caught his breath, I filled him in on the whole story. He then proceeded to tell me that the driver of the truck had been arrested for DWI. Kevin explained that he and Sam were getting a ride back to the cabin, where my car was waiting. They said they would come pick me up in twenty minutes or so.

It felt good to focus on facts and information—it made me feel we were "doing" something. It was good too just to hear Kevin's voice, to laugh. That was just what I needed. But underneath it all, both Kevin and I fought the urge to cry. We still had to keep it together for Sam and for each other.

As soon as I hung up, though, I walked into the hangar bathroom and sobbed and sobbed and sobbed. The reality of what we had witnessed and experienced struck me hard—yet I still had no idea about the extent of Max's injuries.

Once I regained my composure, I called my parents and my in-laws to give them an update on the few details I knew. Then I called Bob, our neighbor at the cabin. I left a message asking him to let our dogs out to pee. We had expected to be back to the cabin in time to let them out, but that plan had obviously flown out the window. So, my strange premonition about needing to tidy up had been true.

Kevin and Sam called to say they had arrived at the hangar. I regained my composure once again before going out to the parking lot to meet them for our long journey to Duluth.

While we drove, we talked about the accident and speculated about Max's injuries. If we weren't talking about the accident, we were answering calls and texts from loved ones who had heard the news. It was only an hour and a half, but it was the longest drive ever.

When we finally made it to the hospital, I felt both relieved and terrified. What had happened since Max arrived? Did he remember we were coming? Was he scared?

On our way to the emergency room, Sam started complaining that his foot and ankle hurt. Upon closer inspection, his foot and ankle appeared to be bruised and swollen. We also realized his feet were soaking wet. We determined he would need to get checked out too, just as soon as we found Max.

The intake nurse took us back to Max's room. Before we completely stepped in, though, the surgeon said, "If you're at all squeamish, you'll want to wait a minute."

Yep, that's my sign. Exit stage left.

Kevin went in while Sam and I waited outside the room. We managed to flag down a nurse, who then took Sam to get his foot x-rayed. Luckily, everything was okay. It was nothing more than some bruising and swelling to be expected from the accident.

Once we knew Sam was okay, we went back to Max's room to get the full report. The surgeon told us Max was quite lucky that we had gotten him out of the ATV when we did. Otherwise, he might have died from blood loss.

Wow! Hearing this made me glad we hadn't known how severe his injuries were when we were out on that dirt road. At the time, we realized his injury was serious, and that spurred us into action. But had we fully known how dire it was, we might have been overcome with fear.

The surgeon went on to list Max's injuries. On his left leg, Max's ACL had torn, and a piece of his kneecap had broken off. On his right leg, he had lost an artery, had a spiral fracture of the tibia and fibula, and had an eight-inch laceration on his calf. We'd learn the next day that his right hand was also broken.

The surgeon then informed us that Max needed immediate surgery to clean out the wound and perhaps close it.

Poor Max. As he lay in his hospital bed, he looked so young and fragile, despite his five-eight,150-pound frame.

I was so thankful to learn Max's injuries could be fixed. I praised God over and over again for answering my prayers. But we weren't out of the woods yet.

The surgery was successful, according to the surgeon—who, as it turned out, had graduated with me from high school. (Small world.) However, the surgeon said Max would likely need more surgery. He told us to get some rest and that he'd consult with his partner about next steps.

Max was admitted into the hospital and brought up to the children's area, where he would stay for the next five days. I decided to stay with him, while Kevin and Sam drove home to take care of the dogs and figure out our game plan.

After everyone left, and after the sweet nurse made us some mac 'n' cheese at eleven thirty at night, I asked Max how he was doing.

He looked me in the eyes. Tears started rolling down his face. It was incredibly tender and sweet. It was one of those moments I'll cherish.

"It's okay," I told him. "You need to let it out. You've been through an incredible ordeal today."

Max went on to have another surgery two days later. We absolutely adored his wonderful surgeon, Dr. Kolmodin, and were incredibly thankful he was the one to operate on Max.

The prognosis was good. Everything Dr. Kolmodin had hoped to achieve during the surgery had happened. Thank God.

After the surgery, Max had several new additions to his wardrobe. On his left leg, he had a full-leg brace. On his right, he had a striking royal blue cast from his groin to the tip of his toes. He had a matching blue cast covering his right arm and hand—except for his thumb and pointer finger, which Dr. K. had left out so Max could still text and play video games.

Every doctor, nurse, surgeon, physical therapist, and occupational therapist who visited Max remarked how lucky he was and that someone must have been watching out for him. I couldn't agree more.

Eventually, we got the green light for Max's discharge. The plan was for him and Kevin to live at the cabin for three months. (I am so thankful Kevin and I have flexible jobs as business owners.) We chose to have Max stay at the cabin so he'd be closer to Duluth, where he would continue his recovery care and physical therapy, and because our home is a two-story, which would have made it harder to care for Max.

Everything was set for Max to stay at the cabin, but first we needed to figure out how to get him there. With his brace and cast, he couldn't fit in our car. Kevin went to get the truck from the cabin, only to discover it had a flat tire.

So we ended up packing Max and all his medical gear and equipment into our RV camper. As we drove, I couldn't get over how much if felt like the day we brought him home from the hospital after his birth. I was nervous, excited, and terrified as I wondered how we would take care of him for those three months of recovery.

Let me tell you, it wasn't easy. It was a long journey. Max had his good days, his bad days, and his I-just-don't-really-care days.

The most impressive thing through it all, however, was his spirit and drive. He never gave up, no matter how frustrated he got. If he couldn't do something one day, he'd just get up the next day and try it all over again. He kept doing that until he could accomplish what he wanted to accomplish.

I learned so much from him throughout this experience. Although I wish the accident had never happened and that he hadn't had to experience such pain and fear, I did realize some amazing things happened because of it:

1. We all got closer and tighter as a family. Especially Kevin and Max, who spent ninety straight days together—most of the time, just a few feet apart.

2. Even though we already knew our friends and family were amazing, we had the opportunity to see *just how* amazing they truly are. Their love and support continue to mean the world to us.

3. We learned not to take even one second for granted during this precious life we've been given.

4. I personally committed to God that I will not leave this life until I have expended all the gifts, talents, and strengths he has given me. I *will* give everything I've got, every day. And when it's my time to go, I'll leave this earth with a smile on my face, knowing I've used up everything God gave me. No more settling for average, baby. I am ready to rock and roll! I've learned what's important and what's not. I can guarantee you,

you'll never hear another coulda, woulda, or shoulda come out of my mouth again.

5. We also learned that pontoons are pretty wheelchair-friendly, and that changing a fifteen-year-old boy's commode bin is a skill we never wanted to master.

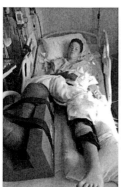
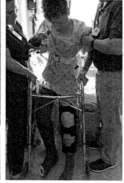

Living with the Lid Up

Lesson

∾

My wish is for *you* to go out and live your life the way you want, so when it's your time to leave this planet, you too will do so with a smile on your face.

Thank you for spending this time with me and for picking up this book. I know there were so many you could have chosen instead. I hope this book has shown you how powerful stories can be—how they can help each and every one of us connect and build deeper, stronger, and more-rooted relationships.

Now . . . go tell your stories, my friend!

Acknowledgments

⤴

I'd like to thank the following people who have made this book possible.

God: You probably know this already—because, let's face it, you know everything. But I want to thank you for creating me and for giving me the strength and courage to put myself and my stories out there. I pray that this book touches each and every reader and brings a little light and laughter into their worlds!

Kevin: Thank you for your support and for always entertaining my wild, crazy ideas over the years (especially this one). You are my rock, my best friend, my favorite human, and the best business partner and propeller-head a girl could ask for!

Max: Thank you for inspiring me to complete this book and for showing me that no matter what life throws at you, you can always find something positive to take from it. You are an incredibly strong young man, and I'm so thankful to be your mom!

Sam: Thank you for always making me laugh, even when it might be inappropriate … which is most of the time. (#creditcard) You bring so much joy and laughter everywhere you go. Keep shining your light, Sammer. You are one in a million!

Mom and Dad: Thank you for always lifting me up and for inspiring me to shoot for the stars, no matter what. I don't know where I'd be without you. Well, I guess without you and that bottle of chardonnay, I wouldn't be here at all!

My friends (you know who you are): I love you all to pieces and cannot thank you enough for your encouragement and your friendship! And a special thank-you to Jessica for reminding me to include a story about the Big Fat Nasty!

Jen Ulrich: Thank you for helping me come up with the name for this book. Who knew that a simple Facebook request would lead to an actual book! #boymomsunite As a special thank-you to you, I will be donating a portion of the proceeds to the Farmington Yellow Ribbon Network in honor of your husband and all the men and women who serve our country.

Ann, Angela, and Kris: You three are simply amazing. I cannot imagine doing this whole "book" thing without you! Ann, you've been an incredible resource throughout this whole process! Angela and Kris, thank you for your killer editing skills, for making me look good, and for cheering me on along the way. #editorsandprintersrock

Rebecca and the Neon Lizard graphic design team: Thank you for designing this book cover and all our social media and website graphics. You're incredibly talented, and I'm so thankful for your intuitive design. #lizardsrule #stillhatesnakes

About the Author

Kari Switala lives in Minnesota with her husband, Kevin; her sons, Max and Sam; and her furry-legged sons, Steve and Murphy. She is also the chief creative officer at Wild Fig Marketing, a boutique marketing firm that specializes in business and marketing automation. When she's not writing or working, you'll likely find her at her cabin in northern Minnesota, where she loves paddleboarding with her puggle, Steve; boating with all her boys; and reading books while relaxing on the dock with a glass of chardonnay.

She is also wildly passionate about helping others tell their stories, so they can better connect and cultivate more meaningful relationships. She does this by presenting her keynote address, "Figstory," to businesses and organizations throughout the country.

Some fun facts: she once rode a cow when she was five, she played volleyball with her intramural college team against prison guards in a maximum-security prison in England, she sang "I Will Survive" with a band in Paris, she hates black licorice and snakes, and she still runs up the basement stairs at Mach speed, because basements freak her out. (You should have seen her do this when she was nine months pregnant—pretty impressive.)